Mary Botham Howitt

Love and Money

An Every-Day Tale

Mary Botham Howitt

Love and Money
An Every-Day Tale

ISBN/EAN: 9783744734790

Printed in Europe, USA, Canada, Australia, Japan

Cover: Foto ©Thomas Meinert / pixelio.de

More available books at **www.hansebooks.com**

LOVE AND MONEY;

AN

EVERY-DAY TALE

BY MARY HOWITT,

AUTHOR OF "NO SENSE LIKE COMMON SENSE," "WORK AND
WAGES," "WHO SHALL BE GREATEST," ETC., ETC.

NEW-YORK:

D. APPLETON & COMPANY,

443 & 445 BROADWAY.

1863.

CONTENTS.

LOVE AND MONEY.

CHAPTER I.

MRS. MORLAND'S ARRIVAL.

" Mrs. Morland is come !" exclaimed Sarah at
Mr. Barker's, the wine-merchant's, rushing into the
parlour where her mistress was sitting at work;
" and you can see the tea-things set out in Mr. Morland's parlour."

Mrs. Barker started up and looked through her
window towards the parlour-window of her neighbour, but the blind was down, and nothing more
than light in the room was to be seen.

" Morland has just brought home his wife," said
Mr. Barker himself, coming with a newspaper in his
hand ; " the chaise has just driven off."

" What sort of person did she look ?" asked Mrs.
Barker, eagerly.

" Like most other folks," said he, sitting down to
the table, and turning over his newspaper.

" Well, but was she tall or short ; and how was
she dressed ?" still questioned she.

" Never looked out to see," returned the grocer ;
" what is Mr. Morland or his wife to me ?"

Mrs. Barker asked no more questions, for she saw
that her husband was out of humour ; so she let him

B

read his paper undisturbedly, and began to make tea, thinking to herself, that, when the shopman came in, she would ask him, for no doubt he had looked out; and then she began to regret to herself that that disagreeable affair about Mr. Crawley's cat had occurred, which had made not only Mr. Crawley, but Mr. Morland and them bad neighbours, for the Morlands were sure to be genteel people; and, after all, the cat did no great harm, though it did come prowling about, and how were they to know that Mr. Crawley had given it to Mr. Morland; but, after all, whether the cat belonged to Morland or Crawley, it was, she must at the moment confess, somewhat unneighbourly to lay poisoned meat for her.

At this point Mrs. Barker's thoughts were interrupted by the three little Barkers rushing in, the youngest roaring with all his might, and the two elder ones speaking at the very highest pitch of their voices; Tommy accusing Fred of having knocked down little Harry, and Fred protesting that it was all Tommy's fault, who would push in to get hold of the back of the chaise which had just driven away from Mr. Morland's. The shopman was sent off to the apothecary's for a pennyworth of plaister to mend Harry's broken forehead with; and the two elder boys, right or wrong, had a psalm of twelve verses given them to learn, to keep them quiet, which set them both a-crying; and poor Mrs. Barker, who had enough to do in scolding the two elder, and pacifying the youngest boy, who was her favourite, gained no information from the shopman respecting the newly-arrived Mrs. Morland.

" Mrs Morland is come!" said Ann, at Mr. Sop-

worth's, the tea-dealer's, on the other side of Mr.
Morland's, as she took in the kettle of boiling water
for tea.

"Have you seen her?" asked Miss Eliza Sopworth,
a lively brunette of two or three and twenty, who
was her brother's housekeeper, and who had invited
that evening Mary Wheeler, the pretty niece of her
brother's landlord, Mr. Crawley, to take tea with
her; "have you seen her; and is she handsome?"

Ann could not exactly tell whether she was handsome or not, but she had seen her sure enough, for
she had contrived to be in the entry when they got
out of the chaise, and she had heard her speak too:
she had heard her say, "and there is a black and
white straw basket, George,"—that was Mr. Morland,
for she knew that his name was George: she seemed
to stand a good height too, and by her figure Ann
would fancy she was handsome.

"And how was she dressed?" asked the young
mistress, eagerly.

Ann again could not exactly tell, for the entry was
dark; but she seemed to have on a black and white
plaided cloak with a large cape, a dark boa, and
some sort of a silk bonnet, but whether it was blue,
or black, or green, or drab, was more than she could
say; there was a deal of luggage, however, that she
knew, besides the "big box," which had come the
day before by the carrier.

Upon this information the two young ladies began
a most interesting conversation, which was no way
abated when Mr. Mark Sopworth, the young tea-
dealer, came in to his tea, bringing with him the
same tidings which the maid had done five minutes

before, namely, that Mrs. Morland was come, but differing from her in some of the minor particulars, as, for instance, that her bonnet was straw, with a black veil, and that she had a squirrel boa and muff; and, moreover, that she had a very pretty foot and ankle, and that Mr. Morland had given her a kiss as soon as she was in the house, as he himself had seen through Mr. Morland's hall window, which was opposite his back shop-window.

Mr. Sopworth looked at Mary Wheeler as he said this; and Mary, who was a very pretty, though somewhat pale girl, blushed very much. Why did she blush?—Nay, how can we tell, for she really did not know herself, and was quite vexed that she had done so. Mr. Mark Sopworth, however, thought she looked so very pretty with that crimson glow on her cheeks, that he placed his chair close to her's, and then went to the tea-table, and selected from a plate of fancy cakes one covered with sugar, in the form of a heart, which he gave to her. Again she blushed, and this time deeper than she had done before, and smiled very sweetly at the same time, which made Mr. Sopworth think, suppose now he were to give her a kiss, what would she say? Would she be offended?

He had almost a mind to try; and perhaps he would have done so, had not one of the apprentices tapped at the window, which was the signal of his being wanted in the shop: so Mary ate the cake, thinking to herself, poor girl, how happy she should be, if Mr. Mark Sopworth really liked her; and her friend the while poured out the tea, and went on talking about the new Mrs. Morland.

"I should not at all wonder if she is handsome," said she, "for he is just one of those men to make a point of beauty. I never fancied him very steady, though," said she; "you know he was a commercial traveller for many years, and those gentlemen always lead such gay lives!"

"Some people reckon him so very handsome," said Mary Wheeler, "do you think him so?"

"Very!" returned her friend, "very handsome! do not you?"

Mary demurred; he came to her uncle's, she said, very often; they drank brandy and water together, and someway or other she did not think him so very handsome; his nose was not straight, and he had such large whiskers.

"A light man pleases you better," said Eliza Sopworth with a nod, and again Mary blushed, for she had indeed thought many a time that, according to her taste, Mark Sopworth was a great deal better-looking than the universally-reckoned handsome Mr. Morland; and, beyond this, she could not help feeling pleased, this being the first time that Miss Eliza Sopworth had ever in any way named her and her brother in the same breath. Very slight things are taken as omens of what the heart wishes; Mary was pleased, and felt that, some way or other, she had never been happier than she was at that moment. "Of course you will call on Mrs. Morland?" said she.

"Oh, yes," said Miss Sopworth, "certainly she should; so would Miss Wheeler; and when would she call? and might not they as well both go together?" Mary said that Mr. Morland had made her

promise to go very soon ; he had told her that she and
his wife would like one another very much, and that
she hoped she should, for that she was always glad to
have lady-acquaintance ; that it was a great deal
pleasanter to her now, than it used to be before she,
Miss Sopworth, came ; she used never to speak to a
lady, perhaps, sometimes from one week's end to
another ; it was such a thing, she said, that her uncle
never made up his mind to marry : she was very fond
of Miss Harris, who was the lady, as Miss Sopworth
knew, whom all the world expected Mr. Crawley
to marry ; and a wife, she really did believe, would
make a very different person of her uncle.   But
seeing, however, that her uncle was not very likely
to marry, she hoped Mrs. Morland would turn out a
nice neighbour, that she did, indeed ! and that she
would not be like Mrs. Nixon, who had always
thought herself too good to associate with tradespeople.

From this they began to talk of the Nixons. Miss
Sopworth had never known them ; they were Mr.
Morland's predecessors, and Mr. Sopworth had been
yet scarcely a year in his shop.   The Nixons, it was
said, had made a fortune there ; he was the inventor
and patentee of various perfumed essences, which had
gained great celebrity.   Mr. Morland, who, as a
commercial traveller, had been in part employed by
him, had, after his death, which occurred before
middle life, purchased his business, his stock in trade,
and his valuable recipes, from his widow ; and, leaving
his travelling, had established himself here as manu-
facturer, hoping, of course, to make as much, nay, a
great deal more, money than his predecessor, inasmuch

as he had a far higher opinion of his own abilities than he had of those of Mr. Nixon.

From the conversation of Miss Sopworth and her visitor, any third party would have discovered that Mrs. Nixon had been a very haughty lady, who had associated only with the wives of professional people, and that it was greatly to be desired that Mrs. Morland might not be like her. Mr. Morland, too, it would have been learnt, from the same unquestionable authority, had taken not only Mr. Nixon's stock in trade, but a deal of his furniture likewise ; Mrs. Nixon had only removed china and glass, plate, and linen, leaving all the rest as it had been when they lived there. It was very good furniture, they said, but Mr. Morland had paid dear enough for it. Becky, too, Mr. Nixon's old cook, lived there still ; Mr. Morland had taken her with the rest of the fixtures. He had a little servant-boy, whom he had put into a sort of livery. Miss Sopworth had seen him only the last Sunday ; and she was quite sure that the Morlands would be very genteel sort of people.

Mr. Morland, Mary Wheeler said, was every way a very different kind of person to Mr. Nixon ; he used always to be down in his distillery in a paper-cap, she had heard say, and a working-dress ; she had been told that he never let any soul see him at work, nor know any of his secrets ; he never used to go out anywhere of an evening, and only just bowed to her uncle when they met. Mr. Morland, however, was quite another kind of man. Old Matthew, who had been Mr. Nixon's porter for so many years, did the distilling now, and Mr. Morland went out somewhere or other every evening—he was a capital singer.

" Oh," she said, " if Miss Sopworth had only heard him sing ' Will Watch,' and ' Oh, Nannie, wilt thou gang wi' me,' she would be delightod!" Mary Wheeler was exceedingly glad, she said, that they had such a neighbour, for her uncle was very fond of his company, and it always put him in good humour to see him come.

CHAPTER II.

WHAT MRS. MORLAND HEARD OF HER NEIGHBOURS.

" Who in the world is that?" asked the bright-eyed Mrs. Morland, from her husband, a few mornings after her arrival, as at nine o'clock they sate together at their breakfast, and the angry, stormy voice of Mrs. Barker was heard outside, scolding her three boys, who were all quarrelling together among the great hop-bags, where they had been at play ; "for Heaven's sake, George, who is that terrible woman?"

" It's only Mrs. Barker," returned he; "you'll get used to her in time, as I have done." And then he began and told the neighbourly history of the white cat which either she or her husband had poisoned. The cat, Mr. Morland said, belonged to Mr. Crawley. They were overrun with rats since she was killed ; and this cat was a capital creature, and very handsome, too. Mr. Crawley had declared that he would not have taken a guinea for her. She used to come into his, Mr. Morland's, premises, and had, it was supposed, wandered after her prey into those of Mr. Barker. However, the cat was poisoned, and was then thrown over the wall down into Mr. Crawley's area.

Mrs. Morland agreed with her husband that it was the most unneighbourly thing she ever heard of; and then she inquired what sort of people they were who lived on the other side of them, and the family, too, who lived at the bottom of the yard; for these, after all, were of the most consequence, because they had all of them but one common entrance-court to the three houses.

"Oh, they are quiet, respectable people enough," said he. "There's young Sopworth, who has the shop and the rooms behind it, and who has been in business hardly twelve months. He is a good sort of person, I believe, though not one of my sort—rather humdrumish. His sister keeps his house, and is a pretty black-eyed girl; his family, who are respectable farmers, live in the country; and the place, on market and fair-days, is overrun with country-folks. All the family dine there on market days, and they are—" Mr. Morland hesitated.

"What are they?" asked his wife.

"Commonish sort of folks," said he, and sipped his coffee. "I fancy he has a bit of a notion," added he, the next moment, "of Miss Wheeler, old Crawley's niece, at the bottom of the yard; she is a very nice girl—quite a genteel girl; but she leads a miserable life with the old fellow—not that he is so old either, but he has all the vices and disagreeables of an old man, with some of the follies of a young one. There's something odd about him; he is a miser and a spendthrift at the same time; a churl, and a downright good fellow."

"Not a very pleasant neighbour," said Mrs. Morland.

" Well enough for that," said Mr. Morland, " but I 've heard that, twenty years ago, he had one of the finest chances in the world of being a rich, an enormously rich man. He was of low parentage, I believe, and was apprenticed to the now rich drapers of this place, Hacket and Smith, who owned and occupied all these premises. They did an immense stroke of business, and employed as much as fifty young men, which, for a country business in those days, was something extraordinary. Crawley, when out of his time, remained there as shopman. He seemed to have uncommon talents for business, and, by degrees, got greatly into the confidence of the firm. Hacket and Smith were both of them old men : Hacket had nothing but daughters, and Smith only one son, who, having an independent fortune, had never turned his mind to business. Old Smith withdrew from the concern, and, at Hacket's death, about twenty years ago, Crawley took to the business. No doubt he had to borrow money, and thus began with considerable incumbrance ; but that, however, is only conjecture. I know nothing about it; only this is certain, that even if that had been the case, single man as he was, never did any one begin life with a better prospect before him. He was fitter, however, as one may say, for a servant than a master ; he managed badly. New establishments in the place had taken the lead ; and in comparatively but a few years his retail business had nearly dwindled away. Upon this he took to wholesale, and had all kinds of schemes of trade. If he did not take many orders, however, the life suited

him very well. It was thus that we first became
acquainted : he is a capital fellow over a bottle,
and never got to the end of his merry stories :
that, however, is his good side ; and even after he had
been more than once kicked out of the travellers'
room, he had his partisans, who defended him through
thick and thin. In a while, his wholesale business
would not pay his travelling expenses ; so he returned
to his shop again, which, even all this time, he had
kept on. I knew the place and all these premises
long before I ever thought of living in them. Nixon
then lived here, and Crawley had the shop which
Sopworth has now ; and his warerooms were those
which are now converted into Sopworth's house. The
whole establishment, in those days, had a most unprosperous look : the shop was full of old-fashioned
goods, which he either could not afford, or out of
stupidity would not sell at reduced prices. He took
shopmen at low salaries, who, from want of address
or character, could not get better situations, and half-
starved them and his apprentices, whom he still
took, not for their services, but for the small fees
which he received with them ; while he drove about
in his gig to get orders from country shops. Yet all
this time he dressed well, and reckoned himself
quite above all other tradespeople, for he still, in his
own imagination, estimated himself by the reputation
of his predecessors. He told a merry story, listened
to a merry song, and sate down among his old commercial acquaintance, as cheerfully as ever, to a bottle
of wine, though, I must confess, that he generally
contrived to shirk his share of the expenses. With
all his bad qualities, however, as I said before, he was

rather liked in a travellers' room ; and whether he be
bankrupt or not, it will continue to be so, 1 suppose,
to the end of the chapter."

" Well, I don't know whether that is quite right,"
said Mrs. Morland; and her husband, without noticing
her remark, continued his narrative. ' Shopkeeping,
as you may think," said he, "did not answer; and
he soon found that even his diminished premises were
more than he required. He had the lease of the
whole at a low rate ; Nixon occupied that which we
now have, and the remainder he redivided, with-
drawing himself to the back, where he has one or two
good rooms, and still pretends to carry on a sort of
wholesale business—though Heaven knows in what
it consists. He gives it out that he has an independent
property ; many people believe so : others think that
his income consists merely in the profit he has made
in subdividing and underletting these premises.
Four different trades have occupied the shop which
Sopworth has, in about as many years ; all quarrelled
with their landlord, failed, and made bad work of it.
Sopworth, the fifth adventurer, was reckoned a bold
man to begin there; but he is like enough, to my
thinking, to redeem the character of the place. He
has got, as if by magic, a capital trade. He is a
thorough man of business, has good connexions, and
his family has money, all which are more than half
the battle with a young beginner. He is sure to do ;
but yet, after all, he is no favourite of mine ; there is
something mean about the fellow that I despise—"

At this very moment old Matthew came up with a
woefully grave face, to desire Mr. Morland's presence
in the distillery. Something had gone wrong ; and

two minutes afterwards, Mrs. Morland heard her husband below stairs cursing and swearing, and pre- sently afterwards a tremendous explosion, in which was heard the crash of glass, a hissing of steam, and the whole house seemed filled with a mixture of hot and stifling smells.

Mrs. Morland was frightened out of her senses, for she thought nothing less had happened than the blowing-up of her husband, and she, too, rushed down with the distracting idea that she was a wretched widow. But Mr. Morland, who was alive and well, was damaged only in temper; and she rushed up- stairs again so happy to find that things were no worse, that she troubled herself neither about his anger even against her for coming down, nor for the loss of the hundred pounds which he declared this mismanage- ment to have occasioned,—merely reading to herself the quiet lesson, "that to be sure she had no business down there, George was quite right, she would attend to her own affairs, and not interfere in his; but," thought she, "it all comes of one's sitting gossipping so long over breakfast. I declare it is now past eleven o'clock, and the things are not taken away yet!"

Mr. Morland looked after his distillery all the day; and she looked again over her new home, and found much in it that required her attention. To all ap- pearance this new home of hers was well furnished: there was mahogany furniture in the dining-room; a Turkey carpet, somewhat the worse for wear it is true, on the floor; a large sideboard, with two new plated waiters, which looked like solid silver, reared up upon it, to say nothing of liqueur-stand, castors, wine-glasses, and tumblers   There were crimson moreen curtains to the windows, and two arm-chairs, one on each side the fire-place; so that, altogether, there was nothing to object to in the room. Then there was the drawing-room, as it was called, up stairs, furnished very properly with rosewood and yellow damask moreen; there was a sofa and a sofa-table; a pair of ottomans with tassels at the corners; there was a looking-glass over the chimney-piece, and Mr. Morland's own portrait, the size of life, with black eyes, black whiskers, black hair, large white forehead, and red cheeks, looking out of a massy-gilt frame at you, go wherever you would. How Mrs. Morland rejoiced over this portrait; it was so life-like, so good-looking, so handsome, as she thought her beloved George to be! She never felt more happy in all her life. She loved him with her entire soul; the house was to all appearance well furnished; he had a good business; they should be rich, and they would be happy; for, thank God!" said she, but not with tears in her eyes—for she was not at all sentimental— but with a happy smile on her lips, and a feeling of success at her heart, "domestic happiness depends quite as much upon the wife as on the husband!"

"We are shockingly off for house-linen," said Mrs. Morland to her husband, a day or two after this, and when she had been informed by the veracious Becky that "for certain sure there never had been any more linen in the press since the time Mrs. Nixon left than she found in it—that is to say, two pair of sheets and four tablecloths, two large and two small; that there were only these, and what was in use; and as for kitchen-towels, Becky assured her that nobody but herself could have managed with only four, and two knife-cloths, as she had done; but then she washed every other day. One did not expect," she said, "everything to be complete in a bachelor's establishment; so she put on as well as she could, for she knew when the missis came, things would be different." Mrs. Morland, therefore, who was a reasonable woman in every respect, took the earliest opportunity of speaking to her husband on this subject; and Mr. Morland, who appeared altogether as reasonable as his wife, replied, " Oh yes, he knew it, they must have linen, but that he left it to her buying;" and then he took up one of the new silver spoons, engraved with what he called his crest, displayed above a German-text M., balanced it on his finger, and said these all were good solid silver. She knew that good solid silver was one of his hobbies; so she took up another spoon and said how handsome it was, and that their table was really handsomely set out, and that she should be ashamed of nobody seeing it, especially when they had handsome table-linen. Mr. Morland, who had been accustomed, as commercial traveller, to dine at the best inns, thought as much of good table-linen as his wife did, gave her unrestricted permission to make what purchases she thought proper. She could get them from Hawkins, the draper, he said, with whom he had a bill.

" I love to see good table-linen," said he, thinking of a good dinner; "and every day a clean napkin," added he, rubbing his hands at the same time, for a couple of well-roasted and savoury ducks were set on the table.

Mrs. Morland thought of the good house-linen she

would buy; and Mr. Morland thought of the good dinner he was eating; and never was a wedded pair happier since Adam and Eve ate their first dinner in Paradise, than were the cheerful-hearted Mrs. Morland and her husband.

＊

CHAPTER III.

THE EXPERIENCES OF A GENTLE SPIRIT.

Mrs. Morland made her appearance at the parish church on the first Sunday after her arrival, and all the neighbours had the pleasure of seeing her going there.

"She wore a dark-blue wadded lutestring pelisse, with a chinchilla boa and muff," said Mrs. Barker to the Sopworths, with whom she was very intimate, and on whom she called that Sunday afternoon.

"Her pelisse was levantine, not lutestring," said Miss Sopworth, whose pew being adjoining the Morlands, was undoubted authority in the case.

"Oh, levantine was it?" said Mrs. Barker, "well, levantine let it be then; but she is not at all handsome."

"Not at all," echoed Miss Lizzy Sopworth, who, from some unaccountable cause, had felt a depreciating sentiment towards her; "she has no complexion at all, and a person of her style ought to wear curls."

Mr. Sopworth, her brother, said that Mrs. Morland walked well, for that he had followed her to church, and that she had a remarkably handsome foot; he had seen her smile, too, and that he thought her handsome ; she had fine white teeth, and very good eyes.

There was quite an excitement through the whole neighbourhood about Mrs. Morland. She was observed a good deal, as being the successor of the proud Mrs. Nixon ; but still more on account of her own personal appearance and handsome dress. The whole neighbourhood, such at least as aspired to any equality with the Morlands, talked all that evening about calling one of the next days upon them.

For three days the little servant-boy at Mr. Morland's had nothing to do but to open the door to callers. There came wine-merchants and their wives, but not the Barkers; there came the principal linendraper and his wife ; the wife and daughters of the first booksellers ; there came the proprietor of the town's newspaper and his lady ; and three professional families, and two or three wholesale dealers and manufacturers. It was established at once that the Morlands were to take their station among the first tradespeople of the place, no little of which was owing to his being the successor of Mr. Nixon, who was said to have made ten thousand pounds in ten years.

Among the earliest callers was " old Crawley," as he was called, although everybody added, in the next breath, " and yet he is not so old either,"—accompanied by his niece, Mary Wheeler. Mr. Crawley was extremely merry, clapped Mr. Morland on the back, and drank Mrs. Morland's health, with an accompanying sentiment, which made her feel both angry and uncomfortable. Her husband laughed loudly, as if it were a capital joke ; whilst Mary Wheeler looked as much annoyed as she herself did.

There was something very quiet and sweet about this young girl which pleased her greatly. "She is really very pretty," said she to the Sopworths, who came in immediately after they were gone,—"such soft blue eyes, and such a sweet complexion! Don't you think her lovely, Mr. Sopworth?" said she, addressing him in preference to his sister, whose warmth on the subject seemed not by any means to equal her own.

"Oh yes, very—very indeed, ma'am!" said he, and looked very conscious. Mrs. Morland remembered what her husband had said of his having a fancy for her, and grew all the warmer in her praise; "there is something graceful about her," said she; "she is quite the gentlewoman, has such propriety of manner, and is so quiet and self-possessed; my husband has often spoken of her, but I did not expect her equal to what I find her."

"Well, of all the people that have called on me," said Mrs. Morland to her husband a week afterwards, "none please me so well as that pretty Miss Wheeler. I am glad she lives so near, for I shall try to make a good neighbour of her; but what a wretch is her uncle!"

Morland, remembering Mr. Crawley's attempt at wit, laughed again as loudly as he had done before; and his wife, for the first time in her life, felt vexed with him.

"You are so over-nice!" said he; and while these words were on his lips, old Crawley came in, to finish, as he said, whatever bottles of wine Mr. Morland might have uncorked. Morland understood wine too well not to prefer an unopened bottle even for his own drinking; so taking his cellar-key, he went down for fresh wine; and his wife, seeing the two gentlemen were thus not very likely to part early, protested that she would send in for Miss Wheeler to drink tea with her.

She did so. Becky made them a fire up stairs, and then they took tea together; and there they talked themselves into a state of very friendly feeling, although their acquaintance was not of many days' standing. They talked about their neighbours; they talked about the country round W——, which was the town where they lived; Miss Wheeler informing Mrs. Morland that the prettiest village in the whole neighbourhood was Sommerton, where Miss Sopworth's father and mother lived—not Mr. Mark's—oh, no! she never said a word about him; and then she informed her friend, in a half-whisper, that before long, most likely next week, if it was fine, they were all to be invited, Mr. and Mrs. Morland of course, because the party was invited for them, to go and spend a long afternoon there. "It was a most charming thing," she said, "to go to Sommerton to old Mr. Sopworth's; they were such hospitable people, and there was such plenty of everything—new milk and fresh butter, and cream and cheese-cakes; she was once there," she said, "in haymaking time, and they had strawberries and cream in the hay-field, and rode, all of them, in the hay-wagon; and old Mr. Sopworth was so merry and good-natured, and Mrs. Sopworth made such excellent gooseberry-wine! Had Mrs. Morland ever been to a farm-house?"

Oh yes! Mrs. Morland had—but it was years ago; and she was too good-natured not to be quite sure that

the farm-houses which she had known years ago
were nothing to compare to that of the Sopworths
of Sommerton!

From people they went on to talk about dress· and
Mary said how everybody admired that of Mrs.
Morland. The pelisse she wore on Sunday was
thought so handsome; so was the silver-gray Irish
poplin which she had on the Monday she first saw
her. The silver-gray Irish poplin, Mrs. Morland said,
was not her own favourite—she had others which
she admired more; she had some rich levantines and
satins—one, a figured one, which really was handsome; and so, after a while, the two having grown
quite warm on the subject of dress, nothing in the
world could be more natural than that they should
adjourn into the bed-room adjoining, in order that
Mary Wheeler might pass her judgment on the things
they had spoken of. It was almost enough to excite
envy to see the many handsome gowns which Mrs.
Morland drew forth from their new home in wardrobe
and chest of drawers once occupied by the proud Mrs.
Nixon, whose apparel, however, Mary Wheeler could
assert fearlessly, could bear no comparison in any
way with Mrs. Morland's.

"How very handsome they are!" said she with a
sigh. "I have a pink mousseline-de-laine and a
black silk, but—" She did not finish her sentence;
and Mrs. Morland, who was brimful of benevolence,
declared that the pink mousseline-de-laine which
she had worn when she saw her first, was the prettiest
thing she had ever seen; and that the blue French
merino she was then wearing was very becoming,
and fitted her so well: "but then," said she, putting

her handsome things back again into her wardrobe, "you are such a pretty figure !"

"This is the third winter I have worn this merino," said Mary; "I hope my uncle will let me have a new one this year. I wish for a morone-coloured dress; I never had such a one in my life, and I fancy it would suit me."

"You would look sweetly in it," said Mrs. Morland, "it is so warm a colour."

It is astonishing how intimate this conversation about dress made them. Mrs. Morland stirred up the drawing-room fire, when they went back to it; and they sate down side by side, with their feet on the fender, and the cheerful firelight shining on their faces, with as friendly feelings towards each other, as if they had been acquainted for years.

"I hope you will allow me to come often," said Mary Wheeler.

"Yes, indeed! and I am heartily glad to have such a pleasant neighbour," returned Mrs. Morland, and that so cordially, that poor Mary was almost ready to worship her.

"I shall tell Lizzy Sopworth how charming she is!" thought she, as she laid her head on the pillow that night; "and I hope they will ask us to Sommerton next week," added she in thought the next moment; and then came in suggestions of fancy, which were not without their charm, as how, if ever she came to be Mrs. Mark Sopworth, it would be so pleasant to live still next door to Mrs. Morland, and she was quite sure,—that she was!—that Mr. Mark would like Mrs. Morland altogether as well as she did.

Mrs Morland's coming into the neighbourhood was

the pleasantest thing that had happened to Mary
Wheeler for these many years; and yet, poor girl,
she was only nineteen : but what we say is literally
true; for many years she had not been so happy as
she was now, and yet the next week passed over and
they went not to Sommerton. Old Mrs. Sopworth, it
is true, had called on the market-day with her
daughter, and had asked them all to go on Friday
but, unfortunately, Mr. and Mrs. Morland had a prior
engagement for Friday, and so it was agreed that
Mrs. Morland herself should fix the day, only with
the proviso that it should be very soon.   Mrs. Morland proposed an early Tuesday; but, alas! Mr.
Sopworth was going to a great cattle-fair in a neighbouring town, so it was again put off.   " Only
deferred," said Mrs. Sopworth, " and pleasure deferred
is not pleasure lost ;" then Mrs. Morland had a cold,
and was confined to the house ; and then old Mr.
Sopworth was so lame with the rheumatism, that
they could not ask anybody till he was better; and
then, alas! it was the end of November, and there
was no moon ; but next week, when the nights would
be light again, Mrs. Sopworth hoped that they really
might be able to make all points meet.

Next week, however, came and went, and the
Sopworths gave no invitation ; and the week following
came Mary Wheeler one evening with her work-bag
in her hand, and a shawl thrown over her head, to
beg that she might sit for an hour or two with dear
Mrs. Morland.   Nothing in the world could be more
à propos, as Mrs. Morland had just determined to
send in for her, as her husband was gone to the Blue
Boar, to spend the evening with some gentlemen

there. She had put, she said, some pieces of what remained of her wedding-cake on a plate, and had given orders to Becky to cut them some nice sandwiches for their supper, and thus they should be as snug and happy as possible. She was busy, she said, hemming table-linen, and she was so glad that Miss Wheeler had brought her work; yes, indeed, they should be perfectly happy!

So spoke the joyous-hearted Mrs. Morland, in the fulness of her own contentedness; but the more she looked at her young visitor, the more she felt assured that she had been crying: there were dark rings round her eyes, and she looked unusually pale. Poor thing! thought Mrs. Morland, who had immense sympathy for sorrow or suffering of any kind, and she felt more than ever determined to like her.

"Why do you try your eyes, dear girl," said she, "with that everlasting backstitching?—it is the worst work in the world for the eyes, and more especially by candle-light."

"My eyes are very good," replied Mary, "and I am used to it."

"I have never seen you about any other work than shirt-making," said Mrs. Morland, taking up the wristband which Mary had just finished; "it is so fine. You are making a set of shirts for your uncle?"

"I am always making shirts, or fronts, or collars," said Mary; "I was doing it this time last year; I shall be doing it this time next year, for my work is never done," said she, in a tone that touched Mrs. Morland's heart.

"Does your uncle, then, require so many?" asked she.

A slight blush passed over Mary's face as she replied, " Yes, I work for my uncle ; I made four dozen shirts last year, and, oh, I don't know how many collars."

" Indeed !" said Mrs. Morland, thinking to herselt that she should not wonder it the old fellow dealt in shirts ; and then she remembered all her husband had said of his various schemes of business, and of his severity and unkindness to his niece.

" But you should not stitch at night—indeed you should not,—young people ought to take care of their eyes ; but," added she, rather thinking aloud than addressing her companion, " I hope he pays well for all the work which you thus do for him."

" He gives me threepence a shirt," said Mary.

" Threepence !" repeated Mrs. Morland, almost laughing at the idea of twelve shillings for four dozen shirts.

" Yes," returned Mary, " threepence for a shirt, let it be as fine as it may ; and if I should leave it to be sixpence, that I might receive silver instead of copper, I should never get it. I have got a save-all, like a child," said she, smiling at her own miserable means, " to put my money in, and then, when it amounts to two or three shillings, I can afford to buy some little trifle or other that I want."

" Poor child !" said Mrs. Morland, in her very kindest manner ; " but for all that, Mary," added she, " you always look so nice."

Why was it that Mary Wheeler could no longer keep back her tears? It was because a kind word affects a wounded heart little used to kindness, even more than a stern one ; and Mrs. Morland's sympathy was like the one drop which makes the brimming cup run over. She laid down her work and burst into tears.

"Don't cry, dear Mary," said Mrs. Morland, wiping her own eyes; "young people ought never to cry, it makes them look such figures; when people get old, it does not matter, but nothing destroys beauty like crying: tears and weeping sound all very fine in poetry, but they do not do in real life."

Poor Mary's heart was too full to think about her looks, and her tears gushed forth like a torrent.

"It will do me good," at length said she, growing calmer; "it always does me good to cry."

"Poor thing!" said Mrs. Morland; "but you really should not though; and yet," added she, "you do not know what interest I feel about you, and how it has always made me love you, when I have seen, as I often have done, that you had been crying."

"Well, it really is very foolish!" said Mary; "and crying, as you say, makes one look very ugly; but I can't help it sometimes."

"Every heart has its own bitterness," said Mrs. Morland cheerfully, and who, though she had been crying, had eyes again as bright as ever.

"Yes," returned Mary; "that is true, but only in degree; few young hearts, I hope, have known as much bitterness as mine has known of late years. I am so dependent, you see," said she, feeling a sudden willingness to pour out all her troubles into the bosom of one who sympathised so kindly even with her tears, "so very dependent," continued she, "I cannot call even my clothes my own. My uncle is so strange-tempered, so violent, so tyrannical, I may

say that it really prevents my loving him as I ought
to do," said she, with a deep sigh, "if he is out of
humour, he is always angry with me, and his way of
punishing me is to lock up my best clothes—for
months, sometimes, I have had only one dress, till I
feel so shabby that I cannot bear myself. He has
now taken my black silk and my mousseline-de-laine,
and I have nothing but this merino and my old
morning frock; and if Mrs. Sopworth was to ask us
to go there, I have nothing to go in but this! I
cannot think how he can do so," said she; "and, oh,
it is a dreadful thing to be so dependent as I am!"

"It is indeed," said Mrs. Morland.

"He once turned me out of doors," continued
Mary; "I was very young then, and could not do
anything for myself; but if he were to do so again,
and I sometimes think he will, I never would return
to him: I would go out as servant, or teacher in a
school, and that I really do think of," said she. "And
don't you think, dear Mrs. Morland, that I might get
such a situation; reading, and writing, and needlework, and geography, and all those common things,
and a little music, I could teach very well. There
was a Miss Smith in the school I went to, who was
not any more competent to teach than I am, and I do
think that Mrs. Harris, the lady who keeps this
school, would take me if it were not for a sort of
connection with my uncle—they think it would offend
him; and therefore, though they are good sort of
people, they never take my part: and in any situation that I might get," said she, "I would try to do
my best,—nobody knows how useful I should try to
make myself!"

"I am sure you would!" said good Mrs. Morland.

"I'll tell you what I once did," said Mary "though I never before told anybody else. I had saved my money till I had four and sixpence; I was very unhappy, and I thought if I could get a situation as lady's maid, or to travel with a family, or as nursery governess, how good it would be; so I put an advertisement in the paper to that effect, but it never was answered: I ought to have repeated it week after week, but, oh dear, it takes such a deal of money to advertise, and then my uncle got into good humour again, and so I am here still."

"Have you lived long with your uncle?" asked Mrs. Morland, anxious to know the particulars of Mary's life.

"Ever since I was ten," returned she; "nine long years! People talk about time being short," said she; "to me those nine years seem as an age! I'll tell you about my early youth, for that all seems like a summer's day."

Mrs. Morland said, warmly, that she wished she would; she should like to know all about her; and Mary, smiling, yet sighing at the same time, began as follows:—"My mother was my uncle's sister: there is still another uncle, but I shall tell you about him afterwards; my father was the master of the Grammar School at Morton, in Devonshire; I don't know what the income was, but it must have been small, for my mother kept no servant. There were two children, and we were twins—my brother Edward and I."

"Oh! that, then, is Ned, of whom I have so often heard you speak?"

" Yes, dear Ned!" exclaimed Mary with enthusiasm, for her affection for her brother amounted to a
passion. " My earliest remembrance is of him," continued she ; " we slept in one cradle, we lived as it
were for one another, it seems to me in remembrance
as if he had his arm always round me. He was but
an hour or two older than me, but he might have
been years my elder, so much of a protector was he
always to me. I remember so well his carrying me
over wet places in the road, when we went out together ; his scrambling up the banks to get flowers for
me, and his climbing trees for birds' nests and eggs
for me ;—oh, he was always so good and so very fond
of me !

" Morton, where we lived, was but a small village ;
and the boys whom my father taught came from
neighbouring villages : they used to bring their
dinners with them, which they ate in the school-room,
and then, between morning and afternoon school,
they used to play. There were some very large
sycamore or lime-trees—I do not know which now,—
which grew around the school and the school-house
where we lived, and under these, in summer and in
dry weather, the boys used to play. Ned was a very
merry, active boy, and as fond of play as any of them ;
but, for all that, he never forgot me, but used to take
care that I had my share of fun as well as himself; or
if, as it often happened, I was poorly and could not
play, it never put him out of humour that he had to
sit beside me, or even sometimes nurse me, instead of
playing. He made all the boys as considerate of me
as he was himself; and when it was cold, always took
care that I had the warmest seat by the school-room

fire. I remember his once beating a boy bigger than himself, because he would not give me some cherries, for which I wished, and which were part of his dinner. Poor, dear Ned!" exclaimed she, with glistening eyes, " there never was such a boy as he was ! Then he was so strong, and active, and handsome, whilst I was weak and delicate, for, as a child, I had weak health. My mother was very delicate, too, and was often poorly. My father was very fond of her—he was all to her that Ned was to me; we were, indeed, as you may think, very happy people. My father was one of the most cheerful, hopeful-tempered men in the world, and had a heart as kind and gentle as a woman's. He was not one of those people who are kind and amiable by fits and starts; he was always so : he was full of goodness and consideration for others. He used to get up in a morning before my mother, and make a fire for her, that she might have a warm room to come to : he used to do all the errands for her in the town, which was three miles off, because it was too far for her to walk; and after teaching in the school all day, he walked out with her on summer evenings, or worked in his garden—for we had a lovely garden, and both my father and mother were fond of flowers. He was a famous cultivator of auriculas and hyacinths; and down one side of the garden were sheds, in which stood stages of those flowers in pots. I can so well remember the garden, with its neat beds of pinks and carnations, and everything in such trim order ! Monthly roses, and a trumpet honeysuckle, grew up the front of the house, which was very warm and sunny ; and one end was entirely covered with ivy, quite up to the chimney. There were two little windows which peeped out from the thick ivy at this end of the house : the upper one was our bed-room window ; the lower one was in the kitchen, by the fire, where my father's arm-chair used to stand—for we were not grand enough to live in the parlour, though we had one. I remember so well that corner, for we children had two stools beside my father's chair, on which we used to mount to look out of this window, which peeped out, as it seemed to us, from a yard's thickness of ivy, and where the birds used to come for crumbs in winter, and nestle all day in the ivy, because it was so warm. How I should like to see that house again !" exclaimed she, interrupting herself ; " and if Ned and I ever come to be rich enough to afford it, we will go there and see the dear old place, as well as two good old relations that we have there, of whom I shall tell you. But to go on—we were, as you may believe, very happy. The country all round the village was pretty, and the people themselves were so friendly ; the farmers and their wives, and the Clergyman and his sister—they and the squire's family were the only gentry in the village—and they, like all the rest, were very kind to us, and came often to look at my father's flowers, and to see my mother, when she became ill.

" My father's uncle lived in the village ; he was the old relation of whom I just now spoke ; he had, I believe, a little independent property, and he and his neat, little old wife, lived very comfortably, although, like us, they kept no servant. He was very fond of music, and from him I had my first lessons. He and the old organist of the church never could agree—I don't know why; but my uncle, Mr. Fielding, as he was always called, used always to shake his head when he heard the organist spoken of. I suppose there might be some rivalry between them, but of that I knew nothing; nor do I, indeed, remember who the organist was.

" My mother sang very well—beautifully, as it seemed to us children ; and I never shall forget the pleasant evenings we used to spend at my great uncle's. We used to be invited to make these visits, just as ceremoniously as if we had been grand gentlefolks, and we had always, I don't know why, our best things put on to go in. My father, too, used to put a rose, or whatever flower was in season, in his button-hole, just as he did when he went to church and carried a nosegay with him, in his hand, for the old lady. My mother used to take my father's arm, and we two children, washed as clean as soap and water could make us, and with our hair smoothly combed and brushed, walked before them, hand in hand, exactly as we used to walk to church on Sundays. There was a something very ceremonial in these visits, and yet they were always occasions of rejoicing. We always went on Thursdays or Saturdays, because they were half-holidays, and we were invited to tea at four o'clock, because they were very old-fashioned people ; thus it was always, both winter and summer, daylight when we went ; and when our neighbours saw us thus walking up the village—for my uncle lived quite at the other end—they used to say, as they met or passed us, ' So you are going to Mr. Fielding's to tea ?'

" We always had hot pikelets, well buttered, to tea. The old lady used to begin baking them as soon

as we entered the house; and when we children had
eaten what my mother thought was quite enough,
she used to say, ' No more, not a bit more, children !'
And then the old lady would say, ' Poor things ! they
don't get hot pikelets to tea every day !'   And then
she put two bits on each of our plates, smoking hot,
and swimming in butter, and winked at us, as if to
say, 'Now get them eaten, children, before your
mother sees it !'   And so it was always, and precisely
the same ceremony and the same words were repeated,
with the little thick squares of seed-cake, which were
handed to us at parting.   ' Get it eaten, children,'
she would say, ' before your mother sees it—or put it
in your pockets ; for I 'll warrant me you 'll be glad
enough of a bit of seed-cake to-morrow !'   At which,
of course, our mother and the old aunt smiled at one
another.   They were dear old people, those !" said
she, luxuriating in the pleasant memory of those past
years—" and they must have been rather well to do
for their station, for they lived so comfortably : and in
winter-time, never let us come away without a cup
of warm elderberry wine. After tea, my uncle seated
himself at his grand piano—a most costly and splendid
instrument, which almost seemed out of its place in
so poor a house—and played for an hour or two ; he
had very great knowledge of music, and must have
played remarkably well.   I can remember even now
what he used to play ; both Beethoven and Mozart
were favourites with him.   He must have spent a
deal of money in music, for he had a great deal ; and
one of the perpetual subjects of complaint with him
was, that people sent to him from far and wide to
borrow music, and that he had great trouble in getting

it back, and even when he did, it was returned to
him dirty. He was very clean and precise himself,
and his wife was just the same. There was a green
baize cover kept over the piano ; and he never closed
it, after playing, without carefully wiping the keys
with a clean silk pocket-handkerchief.

" I learned to play a little from him, and he always
maintained that I had great talent for music. My
uncle Crawley is fond of music, too, and I must
acknowledge that he took care that I should not lose
that which I had already learned. But to proceed
with my history. As a child, you may believe that I
was very happy. Home, with father and mother, and
loving brothers and sisters, how blessed it is ! and our
home was like a heaven on earth. I remember no
such thing as disunion ; there was neither unkindness
nor hardship. Summer and winter, morning and
evening, all had their duties and their pleasures.

" One of the most mysterious ordinations of Providence," said she, after a pause, " is the breaking up
of households like ours ! Slowly, as I can now
remember, did the health of my mother give way.
At first, my father drove her over to the town in a
taxed-cart, which he borrowed for the occasion, to
consult the physician ; and then we children were
sent to our uncle Fielding's, where the two good old
people never failed to treat us—we little knew why
—with more than their usual kindness. After a while,
however, our poor mother became too ill to go to the
doctor's ; he, therefore, came now and then to see her.
We liked at first to see his handsome chaise drive up
to the door, and thought that we should never be
tired of admiring the well-harnessed horse, and the

bright box-axled wheels. By degrees, however, a
fearful sort of apprehension mingled itself with the
doctor's visits; our mother lay in bed, and our father
looked thoughtful and unhappy. He was more than
ordinarily kind to us, nevertheless; but he told us
not now merry stories, as he used to do; he wept
passionately over us, and we saw him weeping, too,
in the garden, where he walked to and fro apparently
unregardful of his favourite flowers, though it was
then the time of the auriculas.

" It is a dreadful thing, dear Mrs. Morland," said
Mary, " when sorrow first takes hold on the heart of
a child! Long and bitter sorrow have I certainly
known since then, but nothing equal to the agony
that weighed down my heart, when my father took us
to the bedside of our mother, and told us that she
was dead! We had taken leave of her the night
before. There was something very solemn in that
leave-taking. The Clergyman was there, and the
doctor, too, and our old aunt Fielding, who had come
up for us. She had cried, but we did not; for she had
promised us seed-cake and gingerbread; and we never
thought but that we should see our mother again
on the morrow, and that she would then, perhaps, be
better."

Mary paused here. She wept at the remembrance
of that last leave-taking. Mrs. Morland wept, too;
and it was not till after a pause of a few minutes that
she continued.

" We were nearly nine years old when our mother
died. It was fine summer weather; the garden was
full of roses and all kinds of flowers; bees were hum-
ming in the thick-leaved lime-trees that shaded the

;chool-house door; everything looked cheerful excepting our father. And yet he went on with his teaching
just as usual ; he worked again in his garden, he
walked out with us, and took us to church just as
when our mother was alive,—the only difference was,
that now, instead of our walking before him and our
mother, he took one of us in each hand. A decent kind
woman lived with us in the house ; the clergyman
and his sister came often to see us, and we went again,
as usual, to visit the old grand-uncle and aunt. Our
father was a good man ; he must, indeed, have been a
pious, good christian, to have borne his loss as he did.

" We children, after our first grief, were certainly
not unhappy, for everybody was kinder to us than
ever ; the squire's lady, herself, sent for us now and
then to the hall ; we were rather frightened at these
visits, and never felt quite at ease till our father came
in the evening to fetch us home. I remember won-
dering at him as I saw him sitting quite unembarrassed
with her, in her handsome room, while she said all
kind of friendly things to him, more especially about
us. Not a week passed without some farmer's wife
or other sending us a present—a goose, a couple of
fowls, a pork pie, or ham, or something or other nice
or useful ; for, after all, there is a deal of goodness in
the world !"

"That there is !" responded Mrs. Morland ; "a very
great deal !"

" And especially in a simple country-place like
Morton," continued Mary, "the kindness of people is
unknown ! But I am making a long story," said she,
" and if I tire you, you must tell me."

" Tire me !" repeated Mrs Morland, " impossible,
pray go on."

Mary, therefore, proceeded :—"About a year and half after our mother's death, in the winter-time, there were great floods,—the river which runs between Morton and the town overflowed its banks —it rose suddenly in one afternoon. It was just at the end of the Christmas holidays, and we children were sent for a day to our uncle Fielding's, while our father went to the town, to buy quills, and such stationary as he required to begin again his school-keeping with. He said he should be back about six o'clock, and was to call for us as he passed the house on his way home. I remember, so well, how the old lady had got supper ready—there was pork-pie, and mince-pie, and there was to be mulled ale for my father, who, she thought, would be cold after his walk, and we children, she said, should have a drop, too, to keep the cold out, before we went home. Supper waited—and waited—and one half-hour went on after another, and he came not; and first we had a mince-pie divided, to still our hunger, as she said, and now a whole one given to us, to keep us awake, for eight o'clock came, and now nine, and our father was not returned. At last, somebody came in, and said that the waters were out, and that nobody could pass the ferry ; it was imagined, therefore, that our father had staid in the town all night, and would return in the morning, by the bridge, and the turnpike road, which was four miles round, but—." Mary could say no more ; she covered her face with both her hands, and sobbed violently.

" He was lost in the waters, which, unhappily, he had attempted to cross," continued she, after some time ; "the ferryman saved himself; but he was lost.

They wanted him to stay in the town, for the night had set in wild and stormy, but he would not, for, he said, he must return to his poor motherless children.

"Oh, it was terrible!" said Mrs. Morland, wiping her eyes, in the pause which Mary had again made; and then handing the plate of bride-cake to her, she said, " eat a little morsel dear, and let me give you a glass of wine."

How kind I will be to the poor girl! thought she, with a heart brimful of kindness, as she went to the sideboard for the wine. Mary took the cake, but did not eat it, and tears chased one another down her cheeks, as she sat for some minutes in deep and thoughtful silence.

" We were thus orphans," at length continued she, "and there was not a house in the village but was open to us. My poor mother's two brothers, our nearest relations, were sent for ; the one, my uncle Joseph, with whom I live, and the other, who had been far less successful in life, a saddler in Exeter, and who had a large family of his own. The clergyman and the squire's lady took the most lively interest about us; Mr. and Mrs. Fielding, the good old uncle and aunt, proposed at first to take me they, however, were old people, although, I believe, still living ; and to obviate the necessity of another change for me, or to secure, as it was thought, a richer home, and better prospects in life, the clergyman, and all the rest adopted, with great apparent satisfaction, the after-proposal of my uncle Thomas, the saddler, that they two brothers should each adopt one of us. Nothing, on his part, could have been more generous ; he had, as I said, a large family, and was not rich.

E

My uncle Joseph gave, I know not why, the preference to me, and he being a bachelor, and wealthy, I
was considered the most fortunate. My uncle Joseph,
who knows how to be gentlemanly, and how to appeal
amiable, won the good opinion of everybody ; he was
invited to dine both at the clergyman's and the squire's,
whilst everybody thought much less of the other
brother.   He was a plain, homely man, and rather
blunt in his manners, and preferred staying, the few
days he remained in Morton, at our old relations',
even to winning golden opinions from the village
grandees.   Edward and I, as you will readily believe,
were heart-broken at parting ; my uncle, the saddler,
gave me sixpence not to cry, and my uncle Joseph
gave poor Ned half-a-crown for the same purpose ,
but we cried nevertheless.   Affection is deeply rooted
even in the heart of a child ; and we had been too
much brought up in love not to feel how dear, not to
say needful, we were to each other.

"I came here ; everything was very different to
what I had been used to ; the town was large, and
the house was large.   My uncle was then in business ;
he had several young men and apprentices; there was
no female in the house but the housekeeper and one
maid-servant; the housekeeper was a coarse, vulgar
woman, without education, but who had unbounded
influence over my uncle ; she did not, however, hold
apparently any situation in the family but that of a
menial, and the house had all that forlorn, cheerless
character, which the want of a female ruler always
gives.   It would, indeed, have been a very wretched,
not to say unfit home for a young girl, had it not been
for one circumstance.'   For many years my uncle had

been supposed to have matrimonial intentions towards a most excellent young lady,—though young, indeed, she then was not,—who, with her mother and sister, kept, and yet keep, a school. She had, it was said, refused better offers out of regard to him, and in the belief that he certainly would fulfil his engagement with her. But year after year went on, and he still paid, if less warm, at least not less constant attentions; but, unquestionably, his matrimonial wishes grew fainter and fainter, whilst she, with the unwavering, unwearying, constancy of a woman, loved him as truly as ever. To her care I was confided as a day-boarder; and, for his sake, if not from real affection to me, she performed her part, as teacher, most religiously. She was an accomplished woman, and taught me all she knew with an affectionate zeal, which soon made it a pleasure for me to learn. She thought, poor thing! to show her affection to my uncle by her attention to me ; and, in proportion as she enabled me to be useful—not to say ornamental—in his house, she lessened the necessity which my uncle had once felt, or had imagined he felt, of a gentlewoman to sit at the head of his table, and of some one to play and sing to him, when in good humour, and to tease and tyrannise over when in bad.

- "Often in my troubles, when, what appears to me, the disreputable conduct of the housekeeper,—who is now our sole domestic,—and my uncle's violent temper, have almost driven me distracted, I have thought of flying to this lady, and taking refuge with her; but calmer reflection, and some little experience, has taught me that that will never do. Much as she and her family like me, they would not run the risk of displeasing my uncle, by taking me under their protection in defiance of him ; or even by letting him suspect that they listen to my complaints. Poor Susan Harris still cherishes the hope of being his wife ; he visits there at least once in the week ; and it is really pitiable to me, to see what an idol he is made among them ; how he is flattered and courted by them ; all the more, as he is cool and worldly ! God knows ! but with all their efforts to win him, it is my opinion they will never succeed, though he himself will still keep up hope, because, to say the least, it still keeps him connected with a respectable family."

"And your brother?" asked Mrs. Morland, "how did he go on ?"

" Yes, poor dear Ned," returned Mary, with sparkling eyes ; " it is my greatest joy to think that he is born to be fortunate. Something or other good always turns up for Ned ; he himself has often said, that his bread never falls to the ground on the buttered side. My uncle Thomas did his duty by him most faithfully. He lived hardly, of course, as the adopted son of a poor tradesman must live ; but he was sent to school, and made the best of his opportunities. My aunt was a somewhat severe woman, a rigid Calvinist, and had very strict notions of duty both to God and man ; she made Ned, however, as happy as she made any of her own children, for she was strictly conscientious, and had great compassion on the poor orphan. Fortunately, Ned was a boy of strong health, and of strong moral constitution likewise, and therefore he made the best even of trouble and hardship ; and amid all kind of kicks and cuffs, both morally and physically, grew up a fine, handsome, and, what is far better, a thoroughly good-principled and warm-hearted youth. My poor uncle Thomas, however, whose one fault was good-nature, unfortunately had given his bond for his wife's brother to the amount of five hundred pounds—and this he was called upon to pay. For him, it was a monstrous sum. He had not five hundred pounds in the world ; my uncle Joseph refused to assist him ; so, all that he had was sold up, and, with seven children, to say nothing of Ned, he was made a penniless bankrupt. It was a most sorrowful thing! All that my uncle Joseph would do was to take my brother till something could be decided upon for him. Ned came here—but before I tell you about him, I will finish the history of my good uncle Thomas. His children, fortunately, were some of them grown up. They were good steady young people, and found no difficulty in getting situations. Some of them were able not only to help themselves, but had every prospect of being able to help their family also. Somebody advanced a little money for the father, and he again began business; but the true help came from the eldest daughter, Hannah. She was, according to Ned's account, one of the most excellent of God's creatures ; not pretty, not accomplished of course, but a bright, cheerful-spirited girl, with a ready hand and a ready will, and a heart overflowing with kindness. She went to live as housekeeper with a lady, the widow of a respectable tradesman in Portsmouth ; before long the son, a man worthy of her, as his after-conduct proved, fell in love with her. He was about emigrating to America, and not only took this young girl with him as his wife, but her whole family also.

They were people, all of them, cut out for emigration; they knew what hardship was, and they possessed the best of all power—the power to help themselves. They were not too proud to work either, and could turn their hand to anything; and the result has been happier than might even have been imagined. The sons and daughters are all well married, and the old people live like patriarchs amid peace and plenty. The mother, too, of Hannah's husband followed them in a few years; and we have been told, by people who have seen them, that the old lady lives, as it were, in the bosom of felicity; and whether she is proudest of her son, or his wife, or her grandchildren, it is impossible to say.

"But this," said Mary Wheeler, "is bringing things down to the present day; I must return back to the time when dear Ned came here, and when I saw him last." With these words she took up her little black silk bag, and drew from it a small bronzed profile likeness of a youth. It was a common kind of thing, glazed in a cheap black wooden frame, but for all that, she gazed on it with intense affection.

"This is a likeness of Ned," said she; "I brought it on purpose to show you, though I never thought of giving you this long history of myself. He is very nice-looking, is he not?" said she, showing it to Mrs. Morland; "only this does not do him half justice."

"It is a beautiful manly face," said her friend, "a splendid face; and a deal like you, too!"

"Oh, do you really think so?" said poor Mary, more flattered than ever she had been in her life before; "if I thought that I were at all like Ned, I should have a very good opinion of myself; but Ned's

eyes are so fine!—he has never cried so much as I
have done," said she, smiling; "and then he has such
a lovely mouth—and there is so much in a mouth!
and his teeth are so white and regular, that really it
is quite a happiness to see him smile. Then he is
such a good figure, too—tall and straight; though he
was but a boy when he went!"

"He has the shoulders of a well-made, fine youth,"
said dear Mrs. Morland, again taking up the likeness;
"and I don't wonder at your being proud of such a
brother."

"But his face and figure," said Mary, "are nothing
to his good disposition and his cleverness—you can't
think how clever he is! he talks so well, and is so
witty and merry; and then he has such good sense
and kindness! I don't know how it is," said she,
"but I do not think there is another such boy as Ned
in the whole world! My uncle said, at first, that he
was to be a draper, and help him in his wholesale
business, for he then had given up his shop. I wished
this at first, but Ned could not bear it; he wanted to
go abroad somewhere; and so, after a deal of persuasion and trouble, my uncle consented to his being
apprenticed to an East Indiaman. It really was very
good of him to consent, and I cannot tell you how
grateful these things make me feel. I would love
him, I would be all that a daughter could be to him,
if he would only in some respects be different to what
he is! But to return to Ned. He has made one
voyage, and was in London for two weeks last spring;
but alas! my uncle would not pay the expenses of
his journey here, so I did not see him. I would have
walked to London if I could; neither had he any

money—at least hardly any. He wrote to me, and
some day I must show you his letters, for they are
very interesting; and he sent me from London this
likeness of himself—it is but a common thing—but it
cost half-a-crown, and that was, he said, all the money
he could spare: he sent it by your husband, Mr.
Morland, with whom he accidentally met, and who
said he was travelling this way, and knew my uncle.
Next autumn, the ship will again return to England,
and my uncle has promised me that he shall come
down here. I hope he will keep his word—if he do
not, I think I really cannot bear it! It is the only
pleasure I have to look forward to; and I would
forgive my uncle any treatment of myself, so that he
will only gratify me in this one respect, and more
especially as Ned prays for it as ardently as I do.
You should have seen the beautiful letter he wrote
to my uncle to ask the favour from him last time; I
thought he never could have withstood it: but he
did! Ned sent another letter for him before he left
England; he told me to read it before I gave it to
him, and I never cried so much over anything in all
my life as over it. It was enough to touch a heart
of stone; but for all that, I dared not give it to him.
I knew my uncle better than Ned did; and I feared
that it would have made him so angry that he never
would have forgiven him; so I burned the letter,
and have only endeavoured, by submission and obedience, to deserve from him this one greatest of all
favours, when Ned returns next year, which, after
all, though it is more for me than all the world, is so
very little for him to do."

She clasped her hands, and looked quite pale as she

spoke, so greatly was she affected by this deep wish
of her most affectionate heart.

" He'll let him come ! Never fear, he will !" said
Mrs. Morland; " he never can have the heart to
refuse you ; I am sure he never can !"

Mary felt a good omen in the cheerful assurance
with which her friend spoke, and began herself to
think, too, that her uncle never could refuse her
again; so they talked together, just as if they had
been old friends, of next September, when Ned would
be here ; and of all the little parties and excursions
which Mrs. Morland would bring about to give him
pleasure. So talked and planned they ; and at ten
o'clock, after they had both of them thoroughly
enjoyed the supper of sandwiches and bridecake,
Mary took her leave, and Mrs. Morland sate down
again to wait for her husband's return, thinking to
herself that she had rarely seen a girl who had pleased
and interested her more than Mary Wheeler; and
remembering that she herself had never all this time
said one word about Mr. Mark Sopworth, as she had
intended to have done.

CHAPTER IV.

A MERRY CHRISTMAS DAY.

CHRISTMAS approached, and the visit to the Sopworths of Sommerton began again to be talked of.
The old gentleman was better of his rheumatism ;
there would be a full moon at Christmas ; and if the
weather were but seasonable, as every one predicted

it would be, nothing could be more charming. It
was no surprise, therefore, to Mrs. Morland, when
Miss Sopworth came in one morning with a magnificent country-made pork-pie in a basket, and her
mother's compliments, and begged that, if Mr. and
Mrs. Morland were not otherwise engaged, they
might have the pleasure of seeing them to meet a
party at their house on Christmas day. Mrs. Morland answered, both for herself and her husband,
" Nothing in this world," she said, " would give them
greater pleasure; and there was no fear whatever
but they would come."

In the course of the day, Mary Wheeler came in
also. She, too, had an invitation; and the animation
with which she talked of this approaching pleasure,
made her still lovelier than ever. She was in extremely good spirits that day, and all the world
seemed to wear a cheerful aspect. Her uncle was
no longer out of humour; she had not only received
again the key of her wardrobe, but the promise of a
new dress for Christmas. She had been used, at
least of late years, to so little kindness and indulgence, that a very little of either made her heart beat
with a pulse, quicker and stronger than even Youth
itself:—pity is it, that hearts such as hers, should
have to bear and suffer! But God ordains it all; and
the sustaining angel of His consolation steps in, sooner
or later, to turn aside the bitter cup, and to mete out
good instead of evil; so we will not trouble ourselves.

Mary wound netting-silk for a purse, which, before
his return, she meant to make for her brother, and
talked all the while about the party which would
assemble on Christmas day at Sommerton. She said

that there would be all the Sopworth family, married and single, and that they were numerous. There was the son, who was a brewer, and the daughter, who was married to a rich farmer, and who had many children ; and there was the youngest son, who was apprentice to a surgeon, to say nothing of Mr. Mark, and his sister, Lizzy. Then there would be the Barkers, she said ; for though Mrs. Morland did not know the Barkers, the Sopworths did, and were very intimate, too. She, herself, did not like them, nor the Pocklingtons either, who would be there also. The Pocklingtons, she said, were farmers in a village equally distant from W— as Sommerton. They lived on their own farm, and were rich. Mrs. Barker was the eldest daughter ; and, beside her, there were two others, Susan and Barbara. Barbara was reckoned handsome ; Lizzy Sopworth thought her so, and they too were very great friends ; some people said, that both families wished there to be a match between Barbara and Mr. Mark Sopworth : she did not, however, know anything really about it—only Barbara and she never were good friends, even when they went to school at Miss Harris's together. She should be very glad, she said, to know what Mrs. Morland thought of the Pocklingtons, and especially of Barbara.

Mrs. Morland thought to herself that she could very well understand, now, why Mary Wheeler disliked Barbara Pocklington, however it might be with them when they were school-girls ; and she resolved, on Christmas day, to observe very narrowly Mr. Mark's behaviour to these two young ladies.

Fortunately, a moderately deep snow fell in the

week before Christmas; strong frost set in at the
same time, and there was no doubt in anybody's
mind of the moon shining through unclouded skies
through all the Christmas week. It was the very
weather for the season ; the carol-singers went of an
evening from house to house, singing, in their pleasant child voices, those melodies, half hymn and half
legend, which are only too much passing away from
our popular literature. Mary Wheeler sate with a
working dressmaker, busied in preparing her new
morone-coloured frock, and could not resist giving to
the little carol-singers, in the cheerfulness of her
heart, twopence-halfpenny, which was all the money
she had in the world.

The frock was finished, and fitted admirably, and
Mrs. Morland said, as she declared everybody else
would say, that it was precisely the colour Mary
ought to wear, and that she never looked so well
before in all her life. Greatly pleased was the poor
girl, as was natural, at the idea of looking so well,
more particularly as she was to appear in the presence
of Barbara Pocklington.

Sommerton lay between three and four miles from
W—, on one of the pleasantest turnpike-roads in
England. What then could be more charming,
thought Mr. and Mrs. Morland, than to walk there
over the hard-trodden, yet crisp snow, with the
bright sunshiny winter heaven above them. Mr.
Crawley was to have driven his niece over in his gig;
but as the Morlands walked, of course, she would
prefer walking too ; so her uncle, in the best temper
in the world, said, that he would take young Sopworth, the doctor's apprentice, instead. It was all

capitally managed, and at eleven o'clock, just as the
bells left off ringing for church, the little walking-
party set out, early enough ; but as they walked they
wished to be in time for a rest before dinner, which
was to be at two.

Everything had a holiday-look in Sommerton as they
entered ; church-service was over, and every house
they passed had its windows garnished with holly,
whilst savoury odours of Christmas dinners, to which
even cottagers were going to sit down—for the squire
had given even the poorest a handsome joint for the
day,—met them at every turn. They walked onward through the village, hungry and happy. The
clipped yews and hollies in the formal little garden
before the Sopworths' house, looked wonderfully
spruce in their winter greenness, amid the general
snowy covering, as if they had been trimmed up for
the occasion. The last half-mile of the way had
been over the fields, and therefore, when they arrived
at the house, they saw that the guests had mostly
assembled : the Barkers' fly, and the Pocklingtons'
gig, and light-green market-cart, stood in the farm-
yard ; and even at that very moment, Mr. Crawley
drove up ! They were certainly late !

Before they reached the garden-gate, somebody,
who had seen them coming, had given intimation
thereof; the house-door opened, and Mr. Mark
Sopworth, without his hat, scampered down the
garden-alley to open the little gate for them. The
lower windows of the house were filled with faces,
young and old, all smiling a welcome ; old Mr. Sopworth hobbling on his sticks, for, after all, his rheumatism was not quite gone, came outside the door to

F

meet them; while the mistress of the house, dressed in lilac bombazine, and a cap trimmed with green gauze, was heard, even before she was seen, with welcomes, and upbraidings for their lateness, intermixed.

They were the last arrivals, and great was the ceremony of introduction. Mrs. Morland, who considered herself the chaperone of Mary Wheeler, had no little pleasure in her good looks; her dress unquestionably became her, it was new and pretty; and, to say nothing of the influence of her good, not to say happy, spirits that day, the walk in the fresh air had given a glow to her cheek, and a brightness to her eye, that made her really lovely. At the first glance, Mrs. Morland preferred her infinitely to Barbara Pocklington. Nor was Mrs. Morland alone in her admiration; there was a vacant chair by Barbara Pocklington, where, no doubt, Mark had been sitting before their arrival; but, though it was left vacant, still he did not take it, but stood leaning with his elbow on the chimney-piece, pretending to talk to Mr. Morland, but, with an eye of undisguised delight, glancing continually at Mary, who was seated on a sofa between two elderly ladies, listening to a long history of somebody, who had the day before fallen sick of a quinsey.

Dinner, however, was announced; and as all things were done with perfect propriety that day at the Sopworths', each gentleman took in a lady, and Mrs. Morland had the great pleasure of seeing Mr. Mark start forward to her _protégée_, leaving the stout and dashing-looking Barbara Pocklington to his younger brother.

We are not going to describe the dinner, though

there is no doubt whatever but that the Sopworths'
Christmas dinner might have served as a model for all
Christmas dinners whatever, that were destined to
come after it. It was, indeed, a capital dinner! and
the wonder was, how people, after they had eaten
and drank so much, could ever think of eating again,
at least for four-and-twenty hours; spite of which,
however, both Mr. Sopworth and his wife did nothing
but protest all the dinner-time, that nobody ate anything; that they feared their friends did not enjoy
their dinner; that they wished it had been better;
but that, such as it was, they were heartily welcome,
as they only wished people would show that they
felt! Amid all the eating and drinking, and the
pressing to eat more, and the protesting that indeed
they had quite done—that they had never eaten such
a dinner before in all their lives—and after Mrs.
Pocklington had declared that she must have the
receipt for the forced-meat balls, which encircled, like
a string of precious stones, the dish of roast turkey;
and after Mrs. Morland had begged for the receipt for
mince-pies, the dinner came to a close. The gentlemen walked out, and the ladies sat and chatted, and
talked of the rest of the company, which was
expected to come in for tea.

When the gentlemen came back to the house, the
shutters were all closed, even though, by this means,
the full moon was excluded. If, however, the glo-
rious Christmas moonlight was concealed from within,
other objects, if less poetical, of an extremely agreeable kind, began to present themselves. The plenti-
ful tea-table was spread, candles were lighted, and
every polished leaf of holly on mantel-piece and in
window, shone lustrously.

Never did anything look so cheerful and inspiriting as the great kitchen, as it was called, and where they had just dined, with its large dresser filled with shining pewter-ware, and all decorated with holly and ivy twigs; its large pendent kissing bush which swung from the ceiling; its chairs ranged all round, side by side; its table cleared away, leaving ample space for dance or merry games, and suggestive of these things at the same time; to say nothing of the young girls laughing merrily, and walking about arm-in-arm, as if, when seen in connection with the swinging mistletoe, to bring tempting thoughts of kisses stolen from rosy lips, or from round and blushing cheeks, to the mind. So looked everything when the door opened, in answer to the loud laughter and talking of the returning gentlemen, and there, actually, as Mrs. Morland came to the parlour-door, which opened into the great kitchen, what should she see, but Barbara Pocklington and Mary Wheeler walking arm-in-arm up and down, as if there were no such things as gentlemen in this world, and as if rivalry, and least of all rivalry in love, was the last thing that could agitate their hearts!

The gentlemen were heard talking and laughing as they approached the house; they seemed to take the door by storm, and entered quite tumultuously. Mary and Barbara walked on still, as if such wild animals as these were quite below their notice; when, behold! just as if by the merest accident in this world, they passed under the mistletoe; and at that very moment, an arm of Mark Sopworth, who had stolen behind unperceived, was clasped round the waist of each, and the audacious young man kissed the cheeks of both girls.

" Oh, for shame !" exclaimed both, starting suddenly away.

" Bravo, Mark !" said half-a-dozen voices; and then
a company of young girls, who had been invited for
the evening, came in with their mothers, bonneted
and cloaked ; and before they were aware of where
they were, or what was going on, all found themselves
under the mistletoe, and declared, every one of them,
" that they never could have thought of such a thing
—that they never were so surprised before in all their
lives; and that, really, the gentlemen ought to be
ashamed of themselves !"

There was such a clamour of tongues, and such
shrieks and laughter, as never were heard in any great
kitchen before, since great kitchens were built ! It
was a long time before this Babel subdued itself
sufficiently to render audible old Mrs. Sopworth's
voice, which kept uttering, " Do, gentlemen, walk in
to tea ! Do, ladies, walk into the parlour and find
seats !" At last, however, one heard, and then
another, and presently the comfortable carpeted parlour, with its great gingham-covered sofa and window-
curtains, received them all ; but then it was found to
be so full, that really it was like a crowd at a fair.
But, no matter for that ! " The more the merrier !"
said first one, and then another, till the sentiment was
quite universal ; so those sate who could find seats,
and those stood who could not, protesting, with all
their might, that if the room were ten times as big,
and brimful of chairs, they would rather stand—
that, indeed, they would !

" Where is my son Mark ?" asked old Mr. Sopworth, from his arm-chair by the fire, where he

sate talking of " fat stock," and "corn-markets," with
old Mr. Pocklington. " He has got the *Mark-Lane
Express* in his pocket. I wonder, now, where he is,"
said he, looking round. " Lizzy," said he, addressing
his daughter, " ask your brother Mark for the
paper."

" Have you seen Mark ?" asked she, from Barbara
Pocklington ; "it 's very odd, but he 's not in the
room."

" I 'm sure I don't know," said Barbara ; " I saw
him come in, though."

" Mark !" cried Miss Lizzy, loud enough not only
to be heard by all the company, but to draw everybody's attention to her.

" Do you hear, Mr. Mark?" said a voice, softly,
behind the long gingham window-curtains, which fell
over the window.

" I hear," returned he, and laughed and rubbed his
hands, as if the joke were capital.

" Mark !" again cried Lizzy ; and just at that
moment a mischievous gentleman drew apart the
curtains, one in each hand, and there stood Mark
Sopworth and Mary Wheeler !

Mark laughed louder than he had ever laughed
before, and so did everybody ; while poor Mary
blushed crimson, and thought that she looked extremely foolish. From that moment, Barbara Pocklington hated her. Mrs. Barker inquired from her
neighbour whether she did not think that Miss
Wheeler had been flirting shamefully all day with
Mr. Mark ; and old Mrs. Pocklington said to hers,
that "she should be very much ashamed, if a daughter
of hers behaved as Miss Wheeler did !"

It was a very merry evening, and games of all kinds were played—hunt-the-slipper, blind-man's-buff, and cross-questions and crooked-answers; and then came the merriest of all—the redeeming the forfeits.

Mrs. Barker, it was voted, was to hold the forfeits in her lap, and Lizzy Sopworth was to kneel before her and prescribe the penalty for each.

"Now, what shall the owner of this do?" asked Mrs. Barker, holding a something in her hand.

"Lady or gentleman?" inquired Lizzy.

Mrs. Barker stooped down as if to look at what she had, but whispered the name "Barbara" into her ear, and then replied aloud, "The owner is a lady."

"She shall go round the company," replied Miss Lizzy, "and inquire from each 'what they would write on her heart, if it were a sheet of paper?'"

"It is yours, Barbara!" said Mrs. Barker, holding forth, at the same time, a small and very pretty glove.

"It is not mine!" said Barbara, who had advanced half-way to her sister, "I believe it is Miss Wheeler's."

"Mary Wheeler, are you the owner of this glove?" asked Lizzy Sopworth.

"It is mine," said Mary, and then commenced her round.

"If my heart were a sheet of paper, what would you write on it?" asked she, in the first place, from Mrs. Barker.

"The words of a song which I have heard you sing," returned she, somewhat tartly, "Behave your-sel' be'ore folk."

"And you, dear Mrs. Sopworth?" asked she, from the friendly old lady.

" What would I write?" repeated she. " Oh, I 'm no hand at writing—I 'd make out what gentleman was highest in your books, and hand the pen to him."

" Well done, mother!" said Mark; and all the Pocklingtons thought Mary a greater flirt than ever.

" And if my heart were paper, what would you write on it, Miss Pocklington?" asked she, from Barbara's unmarried sister.

" I ?" returned she, as if offended by the question; " what would be the sense of *my* writing anything? I would hand it over to Mr. Mark Sopworth."

It was beginning to get quite too personal, and Mary felt confused, especially as Mark Sopworth himself came next. " And you, Mr. Mark?" asked she, almost tremulously, " what, if my heart were blank paper, would you write on it?"

." I would write," said he, in a half-whisper, " all that I wish that heart to feel—what I wish to say yet dare not," added he, in a whisper, meant only for her ear.

" Faint heart never deserves fair lady, does it, Miss Wheeler?" asked Mr. Morland, quite loud, who, having a remarkably quick sense of hearing, had caught every word.

" What did Mr. Mark say?" asked Mrs. Barker.

" Something quite too stupid to be repeated," returned he.

" It was not so very stupid either!—was it, now, Miss Wheeler?" said Mr. Morland, chuckling.

" I need not go all round," said Mary Wheeler; " I am sure I have done quite enough to redeem two gloves instead of one."

The company agreed that she had; and Mrs.
Barker tossed the glove to her, and began crying
another forfeit; never seeing, as our own Mrs. Morland did, that Mark Sopworth caught the glove
instead of Mary; and, instead of giving it to her, put
it into his waistcoat pocket.

"What shall the owner of this do?" asked Mrs.
Barker.

"Lady or gentleman?" inquired Lizzy.

"Gentleman," returned Mrs. Barker.

"He must bow to the wittiest, kneel to the prettiest,
and kiss the one he loves best."

"It is Mark's!" exclaimed his sister, looking at
the cigar-case which Mrs. Barker held. "Mark, you
have heard your penalty."

"That is soon done!" said he, starting from his
chair, and, at the same moment, both Mary Wheeler
and Barbara Pocklington felt as if the eyes of the
whole company were on them.

"No," said Mark, the moment afterwards, "I've
changed my mind—I won't do it."

"You must! you must!" stormed on all sides.

"You shall never have your cigar-case again, if
you do not," said Mrs. Barker.

"Never, as long as you live!" said his sister.

"Then I'll go without it," said he, folding his
arms, as if in token how determined he was to keep
his word; "for where all are so witty and so pretty,
how is it possible to make a choice; and then, unless
I may kiss all round, I'll kiss none." And with this,
Mark unfolded his arms again, and looked first at one
and then at another pretty girl, as if he were half in
the mind to do as he said.

"Oh, Mr. Mark!" exclaimed one, and "Now, did
one ever!" exclaimed another, and "Don't let him
have his forfeit back!" exclaimed half-a-dozen at
once; and then amid all this confusion of tongues and
laughter, supper was announced.

Three or four gentlemen sang songs after supper,
among whom Mr. Morland figured to the greatest
advantage; and then three or four ladies did the
same; and then, so enthusiastic did the whole company get, that they all sang in chorus.

"Would you really believe it!" at last exclaimed
Mrs. Morland, looking at her watch, "that it is
actually half-past two?"

The Sopworths declared that that was not late,
and everybody else protested, that never before in all
their lives had they heard of such a thing! that it
was shockingly late; that they ought to be quite
ashamed of themselves, and twenty other such
things.

It took a long time to cloak and bonnet such a large
company; and it took a long time, too, before the
flies, and gigs, and shandrydans were all brought out
of the yard, and drawn up to the garden-gate. The
Morlands had a fly sent from the town to fetch them;
and of course Mary Wheeler went with them, while
young Sopworth, the doctor's apprentice, who was
obliged to be back that night, returned, as he went,
with old Crawley in his gig.

"You can make room for me, too, cannot you?"
said Mr. Mark Sopworth, buttoning up his great-coat,
and coming up to the Morlands' fly-door.

"You are not going to-night, Mark!" exclaimed
his mother and sister, who both stood at the garden-

gate, with candles in their hand, although the moon shone bright.

" We can give you the seat which you will like above all others," returned Mr. Morland, who smelt prodigiously strong of wine and brandy-and-water— " the seat opposite Miss Wheeler."

Mark sprang into the carriage ; his sister said it was too bad that he left her to walk alone in the morning ; the carriage-door was shut, and off drove the Morlands, not a little pleased with their Christmas-day's entertainment.

" Poor Mr. Mark !" said Mrs. Morland, a few days afterwards, and when Mary and she next met, " he lost his heart on Wednesday evening, and you lost your glove."

Mary smiled, and blushed, as she always did, and then, loosening the strings of her black silk bag, took out a neat little packet, which appeared to have been sealed ; it contained a really beautiful pair of French kid gloves. " I wanted to show you these," said she, opening the little packet ; " Mr. Mark sent them to me with a note ; he had lost mine, he said, and sent me these instead ; it is a good exchange for me, for mine were not new ;—and then, really, it was so nicely done !"

" Everything is nicely done, that is done by those we love," said Mrs. Morland ; " but, really, these are beautiful gloves," said she, looking at them ; " and, I dare say, there was something *very* particular in the note—now, I hate mysteries, so you must tell me all about it, for I see, by your blushes, that you have something to tell."

" Oh, no," said Mary, looking crimson as a red

rose, "Indeed I have nothing so very particular to
tell you. There was this with the gloves, and that
was all."

Mrs. Morland opened the gilt-edged sheet of note
paper which Mary handed to her, and read, in a very
neat tradesman's hand, four lines, meant to be poetry,
in which "heart" rhymed with "smart," and "glove"
with "love." She felt rather disappointed that it
was not a direct declaration of love ; but never doubting but that that, too, would come in due season, said
it was very pretty, and that she was sure Mr. Mark
would set quite as much, if not more, store by the
old glove than she would by the new ones.

CHAPTER V.

A RETURN IN KIND.

" WILL you, dearest Mrs. Morland," said Mary
Wheeler to her one evening, not very long after the
Christmas entertainment, which we have chronicled
in our last chapter, " tell me something about your
early life and experience ?"

" Heaven bless you, my dear child !" said Mrs.
Morland, " I have nothing in the world to tell !"

" Nor had I," returned she ; "and yet you said that
you found that which I told you interesting ; do talk
about yourself to-night, or I shall be ashamed of
what I have done, and think I wearied you by talking so much about myself."

" If it is on this condition," replied Mrs. Morland,
smiling, " I will tell you all that by any possibility I

can remember about myself, just to prove with what delight and good-will I listened to you.

"My father, then, you must know, was curate of a rich living in Cumberland,—the living was rich, but he was only a poor curate. This parish was large, and the population, though scanty, was widely scattered; and as my father desired conscientiously to perform his duties as pastor of his people, his life was one neither of ease nor indulgence. He was a singularly learned man; and had he been a bishop, or even a wealthy rector, he would no doubt have made his name famous among the scholars of the age. In many respects, however, my father was not a happy man; he had expected preferment in his younger years; he had been promised it, but had been disappointed; he had hoped and hoped, but in his middle life he was only a curate still; and, somewhat soured with the world, but yet with the elements of satisfaction in himself, had fortune only favoured him in other respects, he settled himself in his curacy, and devoted himself, body and mind, to study, which soon became his greatest earthly delight, and thus found enjoyment in his books, and peace of mind in the performance of his pastoral duties. The misfortune of my father, however, was not his worldly disappointment, but his having married a wife unfitted for him. She was in every respect a worldly woman; and, courting distinction in the world, despised my father, who seemed contented with his humble lot. Had my father been a stern, overbearing man, or even in degree less amiable and yielding than he was, he would have gained more respect, if not more affection, from my mother As it was, they were singularly unhappy, and the remembrances of my early life, unlike yours, Mary, are of domestic disunion and bickering. But we were poor—of that there is no doubt; and I have always found," said she, "that though fortune may, and does, no doubt, bring with it its train of discontents, no discontent, no wear and tear of temper, is like that which a narrow income brings with it, and especially when there is one member of the family troubled by ambition and love of show, as my poor dear mother was. My father promised, that in case his family was large, he would again sue for preferment, or at least increase of income; but year after year went on, and though he said he would do it, he never did; my mother could not understand his feelings on this subject, and had no forbearance with him. Poor man! the sanctuary to which he fled from all his vexations, worldly and domestic, was his study; there he passed most of his time, and there I believe he was happy. His books were his true friends; they had not deceived him; they counselled him in trouble, and infused gladness into his wearied spirit.

" Years went on, and he lived in a world of his own, out of which when he came, he looked like one of the Seven Sleepers awakened. The family consisted of five boys and myself; and my father, as well as my mother, saw the necessity of something being done for us; and, to better his income, in a way much easier than suing from the great, he took to authorship. It was exactly the life for him, as it furnished him with the most plausible and best of all possible excuses for shutting himself up in his study; but, alas! though he wrote books without end, they

were such as nobody read, and, worse than all such
as nobody bought.

" In many respects, there were points of resem-
blance between my poor mother and good Mrs. Prim-
rose, in the Vicar of Wakefield. Among other things,
she aspired to intimacy with the great ; she would
visit with the scattered gentry of the neighbourhood,
and scorned all under the pretension of esquire ; she
knew her husband to be a learned man, and she
expected fame, if not fortune, from his works. Such,
at least, were her earlier aspirations. But disappointment on disappointment cools the most sanguine-
hearted ; and, alas! not only cools, but often embitters
also. It was so in my poor mother's case : unable to
visit with the rich, she despised the humbler class, and
thus came to be disliked by the parishioners. From
her upbraidings, my father took refuge in his study,
and buried himself still deeper in his books. Often,
for days and days, not a word passed between my
parents ; my father forgot, or seemed to forget, his domestic annoyances there ; and this, to an irritable tem-
perament like my mother's, seemed an additional wrong.

" My five brothers ran wild like untamed colts ;
my mother thought and said, that, as boys, they were
my father's charge, whilst I, as a daughter, belonged
especially to her ; and to me she unhappily soon
looked as to the future prosperity of the family.
Poor thing ! she fancied me handsome, and a genius,
and God knows what ! I was as fond of reading as
my father himself, and the circulating libraries of
the neighbouring town furnished for awhile food for
my inexhaustible appetite. I drew, as all lively
children do, and my scrawls were exhibited as mira-

cles of genius ; music I began to learn, but too impatient to advance, step by step, in that most difficult of
sciences, I composed vagaries of my own, and at
thirteen set up for a musical composer.

"I was, as you may imagine, ignorant, vain, and
overbearing, and must, indeed, have been a most
detestable child.   Our respectable neighbours, offended by my poor mother's pride, looked on me, as was
natural, with pity, if not contempt.   They were
homely people, who thought homely virtues and
homely knowledge the most estimable things in life,
and they had justice.   For myself, I was helpless as
a child, in the common business of life ; my mother
blindly doting on me, as she did, permitted me to
take no part in household work ; everything was done
for me, and that by my mother, for my time, she
believed, was much better employed in those accomplishments, in which I was, and never could be other
than the merest dabbler, than in learning either to
help myself or others.   Unfortunately, too, as I said
before, she had a great notion that I was handsome,
and that my face, if my genius failed, must make all
our fortunes ; all needlework, therefore, was prohibit-
ed, lest I should spoil my eyes, or injure my figure
by stooping.   I was permitted to do no household
work either, lest my hands should become coarse and
red.   It was in vain that my poor father now and
then woke up, as it were, from his books, and
objected to my mode of education : ' Why does not
Ellen mend the boys' stockings ? why does not Ellen
do this, that, and the other?' he would inquire ; and
then my poor mother, stung by questions which were
not easy to answer, grew angry, and, in her turn,

upbraided him with the untamed wildness of her
sons, who, early in life, had given both parents cause
of uneasiness.

"We were an unhappy, disorganised family; and
my brothers seemed likely enough to bring lasting
disgrace on the family, if not on the clerical name
also ; add to which, long accumulated debts threat-
ened to conduct my poor father to a prison. In this
crisis of affairs, the parishioners complained, I believe,
to the rector; the bishop interfered, and my father
was in a fair way of losing his curacy.

"Ruin stared us in the face; I was then nearly
seventeen, and my eldest brother nineteen ; we were
like people overtaken at once by shipwreck or fire ;
we looked on and around, and there was nothing but
ruin and dismay.

"My mother had a brother, a tradesman, in Bristol,
a well-to-do man, who often, in reply to her complaining letters, had sent her a ten or a twenty
pound bill. To him, of course, application was
made in our distress ; and in reply to my mother's
letter, instead of writing, he came instantly. Never
shall I forget his arrival, and the influence of his
presence ! We were all dreamers, as it were, and all
our actions were characterised by indecision. 'What
is to be done? what is to become of us ?' exclaimed
my poor mother, distractedly. 'Done !' repeated my
uncle; 'why, work ! Are not these young people,'
asked he, 'endowed like the rest of their kind?—
hands have they, and heads—what would they have
more ?'

"Three of my brothers he sent off in a few months'
time to Australia, with a hundred pounds each ; and

there, with ample space for their wild energies, they
have done well. Me, without asking even leave of
my parents, he took to live with him, as his own
housekeeper. Nobody thought, I believe, of object-
ing to anything he did : he settled all as with a '
moment's thought ; but the truth is, he had come
with plans ready arranged, and it never entered his
head that things could be better than he arranged
them ; nor indeed could they.

   " He staid with us a fortnight, and in that time
wrought a complete change in our affairs. He went
from house to house, among the parishioners, and
everywhere he dropped, as it were, a seed of goodwill
and forbearance. He went, also, quite unsolicited by
my parents, both to the rector and the bishop, and
said so much in my father's behalf, as excited their
sympathy and kindness towards him ; the end of all
was, that he was re-established in his curacy more
firmly than ever ; besides which, though he was not
able to gain an augmentation of his salary, he made
some little addition to his income from his own purse.
But that which, after all, was most to the purpose was,
that he roused my father from his learned lethargy,
to feel and to see the kindness and the goodwill of
those around him ; and to make my father feel this
was to give a new impulse to action, and a new value
to life. My mother made no objection to anything,
not even to my leaving her ; but I had been, it is true,
but of very little use to her. I could do, comparatively speaking, nothing ! and my uncle said that my
absence was better for her than my presence, at least
for some time ; and that when I returned to her, if
I were fit for nothing better, I should be fit for a
respectable man's wife.

"My uncle was a very peculiar person, but one of the wisest and shrewdest of men. He accomplished that which he desired, however improbable it might at first seem, not so much by a *coup-de-main*, as by calmly sapping and mining, and never being turned aside, or daunted by any impediment whatever; such had been his course through life, and thus he went to work in our affairs. It was thus that he operated with my father's parishioners and patrons; he did not present himself as his violent partisan and upholder through right and wrong, overpowering his opponents by many strong words and arguments, to prove my father faultless: no! but all the while that he was conceding and agreeing, and letting people think that they were having everything their own way, he was, by the few kind, wise words which he let fall in the right place, winning more good-will for my father, than anybody but himself supposed. It was so with my parents themselves; he never seemed to blame either one or the other of them, nor yet did he set about to convince them either of this or that; and yet he ended by making them think exactly with himself, and take different views of life, and its business, to what they seemed to have done before; and if they did not, hereafter, always act in concert, at least they dated a new era of domestic happiness and comfort from that time. It is remarkable, that after then, my father wrote no more books, and my mother condescended to visit such families in the parish as did not write esquire to their names. My three elder brothers, as I told you, have all become respectable men in their colonial life, and, of my two younger ones, the one is in my uncle's service, and the other has taken a bachelor's degree in the University of Cambridge."

"And with yourself," said Mary Wheeler, "it must have gone equally well."

"Yes," said Mrs. Morland. "But only think of me, a romantic, inexperienced girl, ignorant as a child of every-day business, with the notion that I was handsome, and a genius, and, heaven knows what of other absurdities, brought at once into a large house, and being told that I must consider myself as the mistress of it; that much would be required from me, and but very little excused! I was, indeed, frightened almost out of my senses ; and yet, on our journey to Bristol, which was made leisurely, in order that I might see something of the country, and the places through which we went, he had so far excited my respect, not to say reverence, for him, that I accepted my office, sincerely determined to do my best. My uncle did not, as so many would have done,—who, with half his acuteness must have seen what a poor creature I was,—humble me, and depreciate what little knowledge I had ; on the contrary, he gave me credit for all the knowledge which I ought to have possessed, and, when I blundered and failed, he purposely shut his eyes. What he saw of arrogance and folly in me, and, heaven knows! he must have seen a deal, he never spoke of it, or even reproved it, but, by the most extraordinary tact, set things before me at once in their true and most beautiful light. I was humbled, but ennobled at the same time; a new life, useful, and good, and real, seemed opened before me, in which I longed to become an actor. He was satisfied to awaken the better part of my nature, without asking my confidence. I made, thus, no confessions, either of regret for the past, or of resolve for the future; but esteem and affection filled

my heart, and they did most to make my good reso-
ntions effectual.

"However much my uncle must have blamed my
parents, and especially my mother, for my faulty
education, not one word was ever spoken by him
to their disparagement; on the contrary, he used
all his endeavours to keep alive our family affection, and was very exact in my writing regularly
home."

"What an excellent man!" exclaimed Mary
Wheeler.

"Excellent, indeed!" returned Mrs. Morland.
"Spirits such as his are the very salt of the earth. But
to continue my narrative :—'On the last stage of our
journey, my uncle first began to speak of that which
he had done for my family. I expressed my gratitude
with tears. 'I mention this only,' said he, 'in order
that you may understand why your duties in my
house are as arduous and responsible as you will find
them. Hitherto, I have kept a hired housekeeper ;
I cannot afford that longer; you must supply her
place, and thus you will confer real service on me.
The keys of all that my house contains will be put
into your hands. I require order, regularity, and
propriety; without these I cannot live. You will
endeavour to please me, and you will succeed.'

"My uncle's manner was always so firm yet calm,
that, while it excited no opposition in the mind of
the hearer, it had the power of assuring and of
inspiring self-respect. Thus it was, that I was not
discouraged on entering on my new, and, really
responsible duties, ignorant and inexperienced as I
had come to know myself; nor, though I was, at

first, almost too anxious, and too much frightened to
sleep, did I despair of succeeding in the end.

"A large house, as I told you, was put under my
charge. I had two servants to manage, and a household of five persons, independently of servants, to
provide for. I found, however, order and precision in
the whole establishment. 'A place for everything,
and everything in its place,' was my uncle's watch-
word. He took me over the whole place the day
after my arrival ; showed me into every chest, and
drawer, and closet, of the house, and, in a few clear
sentences, laid down a plan of household management
for me. He had the rare, but great gift of expressing
himself in very few words; and thus all was clear and
definite from the beginning. My heart almost died
within me, when I saw that which devolved upon me,
more especially when, in a few days' time, my uncle
brought a piece of linen—which I had to make into
shirts, and wool—which I was to knit into stockings,
and table-linen—which I had to mark. I was un-
skilled with my needle, and, strange as it may seem,
could neither back-stitch nor make button-holes,
and as for knitting—I hardly knew how to hold my
needles. Not the least notice, however, did my uncle
take of the consternation depicted in my countenance,
but only remarked, that he was in no great hurry for
these things ; if all were done in a year's time, that
was enough. I suspected, what was really the case,
that my uncle knew how woefully ignorant I was of
these common things, and I was piqued to let him
find me cleverer than he imagined. I practised my '
ne dle, therefore, in private; unpicked the whole of a
shirt, that I might the better understand the making

of one, and, in process of time, felt not a little vain in
seeing the work proceeding regularly and well, in
his presence.

My uncle spent his evenings mostly at home ; a
youth, whom he hired for the purpose, came in
regularly from six till nine to read aloud to him.
Newspapers, history, and travels, were his favourite
reading ; and whilst he listened he drank his coffee,
which was his favourite beverage. He required me
to be always present at this reading, and to employ
myself the while at needlework.

" All the powers of my genius ceased the moment
I entered my uncle's house. I neither drew, nor
painted, nor composed music. I wrote neither poetry
nor romances ; nor had I time to read those written
by other people. Someway, I don't know how, I
lost my relish for these things ; I despised my own
miserable attempts at the whole range of the fine arts,
and, like an appetite which has been satiated with
sweets, I turned with ten-fold relish to solid and
substantial things. I mentally hungered and thirsted
after strengthening literature and improving knowledge. My whole being seemed to respond to my
desires ; whatever I did, or heard, or saw, seemed to
unfold new and ennobling views of life, and to make
that clear which had been hitherto dark and confused.
My heart was cheerful in the consciousness that my
life was and would be useful ; and every day developed
powers in me of which I had had no conception,
and which I had hitherto envied in others.

" You must not, however, imagine, dear Mary,"
said Mrs. Morland, " that, with all my ignorance and
inexperience, my uncle had nothing to excuse or over-

look. I'll tell you," said she, laughing merrily,
" what an affair I made of the dinner I first arranged
and cooked for my uncle and three gentlemen, friends
of his. ' Now, my dear,' said he, ' to-morrow I bring
three gentlemen to dinner; I wish something plain
and nice—soup—a roast—something boiled if you
will—and a pudding ; that is quite enough.' I had
no cook ; all devolved upon me, and I was determined
to do something quite super-excellent. By some
means or other, however, I quite forgot the soup, and
thought only of the roast and the boiled. I considered
with myself what my uncle liked the best ; I
knew that veal was in season, and that it was a
favourite dish with him—so I bought a handsome
leg of veal, crammed it, someway or other, full of
stuffing, and roasted it whole—think only of a whole
leg of veal! I boiled the most beautiful tongue I
could find, and the finest new potatoes and cauliflowers ; all of which I cooked by the most approved
receipts in the cookery-book. A bread-pudding, too,
I made—not forgetting wine sauce—and an apple-
tart. It was not at all a bad idea of a dinner ; and I
never felt better pleased in my life than when,
punctually as my uncle and his friends entered the
house, I saw my leg of veal, richly browned, and
done to a turn. It was, as I thought, a magnificent
joint, which the very largest dish in the best dinner-
service was hardly big enough to hold : the tongue
smelt savoury, the potatoes were mealy, and the
cauliflower unbroken and delicate. I anticipated for
myself unmingled glory, and hastily changed my
dress to take my place at table, thinking with myself
that if the pudding would but turn well out of the

mould, I should have achieved for myself great honour
that day! This great big dish, for which we had not
a cover large enough, was brought in and set before
my uncle; the tongue was set at the bottom of the
table, and the vegetables on each side.

"'But the soup?' said my uncle, glancing at me.
I felt as if a thunderbolt had struck me; I don't
know whether I turned pale or red, but all at once I
remembered that I had forgotten the soup. 'So
then,' said my uncle, interpreting my silence aright,
'there is no soup!'

"The ill-fitting cover was taken from the dish, and
I saw at once a smile on every countenance. I saw
that I had again done wrong, and I was mortified and
ashamed! 'I hope your veal is done,' said my uncle,
as I thought, rather sternly; and all at once it struck
me—of which I had never thought before—that people
did not cook legs of veal whole. I thought of legs
of mutton and legs of lamb, but I could not console
myself. 'What will become of me,' thought I, 'if
my potatoes and cauliflowers are wrong also!' My
apple-pie I felt sure was a failure, and my pudding
would stick to the mould. 'What a responsible thing
cooking a dinner is!' thought I, and was ready to
burst into tears.

"Whether the veal really was thoroughly done or
not I cannot tell, but my uncle and his friends said it
was excellent; they praised the tongue, too, and the
vegetables; and though the pudding did not turn out
perfectly, and I was obliged to confess to myself that
the apples were not quite done, still all ate heartily
and seemed so good-humoured, that even I might
have been reconciled to myself. But that was not so

easy. I knew that I had failed; that the dinner, after all my efforts, was ridiculous; and, leaving my uncle and his guests to enjoy their wine, I went into my own room and cried bitterly.

" Not one word, however, did my uncle say about it. I was terrified when he came to breakfast next morning, but he read his newspaper just as usual; and had I not known him too well for that, I should have imagined he either did not care about it, or had quite forgotten it.

" ' Ellen,' said he, in about a month's time, ' I shall have six friends to dine with me next week; let all be properly arranged. I will write down what I wish for dinner, and mind that all is done well.'—' Might I only just for once have a hired cook, or somebody to direct me?' said I, full of apprehension and terror. ' No, no,' said he, good-humouredly, ' you must learn to rely upon yourself; you will not again roast a whole leg of veal.'—' Oh, for Heaven's sake, dearest uncle,' exclaimed I, ' do not mention it; I am ready to cry whenever I think of it!' "

" And how did you succeed this time?" asked Mary.

" I begged my uncle," returned Mrs. Morland, " to give me immediately a list of the dishes he wished; and whatever was new to me, or about which I was not confident, I made trial of for the dinners which intervened; and this time all succeeded well. My uncle was greatly pleased; I was put in good humour with myself, and never feared, and never very greatly failed, after that time.

" A few years, as you may believe, made a very great change in me. I was as practical as my uncle himself, and was well skilled, if not clever, in all that was useful and domestic, and as far as character and views of life went, if I had been judged by these, my own mother would not have known me.

" The income which my uncle allowed my parents enabled them to live much more comfortably, and to maintain my youngest brother, as I have said, at the University. My parents wished that I should return to them, but my wishes were adverse to it; I was not necessary at home, and I flattered myself that I was so to my uncle. My uncle was greatly pleased by my decision, and his kindness to me increased daily; unhappily, however, my mother was hurt by my refusal, and this was most painful to me. Time slid on—I was now seven-and-twenty; and one of my uncle's sons, who was happily married, wished to become, with his wife, an inmate of his father's house. This was most desirable to me, as I had then become acquainted with Mr. Morland, and he was impatient for our marriage. My uncle, who in goodness and consideration is superior to all other men, made me a present of three hundred pounds, one of which he insisted on my laying out in preparation for my marriage, and counselled me to return for a few months to my father's house, that a perfectly good understanding might exist amongst us, that my father might unite us, and that I might begin my married life with his and my mother's blessing.

" Such, dearest Mary," said Mrs. Morland, " has been my life; there is no romance in it; but please God only that I rightly make use of the lessons it has given me, I shall not be altogether useless in my sphere, be it large or be it small."

CHAPTER VI.

WHATEVER the party at Mr. Sopworth's on Christmas-day might think of Mary Wheeler, and her
flirtation with Mark Sopworth, as the Pocklingtons
all called it, the impression which Mrs. Morland
made on every one was extremely favourable. She
was unanimously said to be handsome; her dress was
admired, and altogether, she was declared by everybody "one of the genteelest people they ever saw;"
and to be "quite an acquisition to their acquaintance."

Accordingly—spite of the tragical history of the
white cat, and spite of Mrs. Morland being so intimate
with that "flirting thing," Mary Wheeler—Mrs.
Barker commenced an acquaintance with her, and
determined not to let it die away for lack of very
frequent calls on her part, and by showing her good-
will in bringing all the news and gossip of the neighbourhood.

Months went on, and Mrs. Barker came in one
summer afternoon, brimful of news about old Mr.
Crawley. "Was it not a shocking thing?—and had
not she really heard?—and this was not the first
time he had been arrested;—his name would certainly
be in the Gazette before this time next year; and then
what was to become of Miss Wheeler? for it was certain sure that Mr. Crawley's lease had only a few
years to run, and his creditors would take that as

property ; it would be sold, and then, maybe, Mr
Morland would buy it; or perhaps Mr. Mark Sopworth—the Sopworths were very rich people. Mr.
Mark had already had a thousand pounds from his
father to begin business ; it was all nonsense about his
ever marrying Miss Wheeler; his family, she was sure,
would be very angry if he did ; she did not doubt
but that she would jump at him ; she was always
flirting with him ! Did not Mrs. Morland, now,
honestly think her a flirt ?" "No !" "Well, now,
that was odd ! Mrs. Morland was the only person
who did not think Mary Wheeler a flirt ; and then
so affected ! She comes into a room with her head on
one side, and if anybody looks at her, she blushes—
all coquetry and affectation ! Mrs. Barker hated
coquetry and affectation, but she knew what she knew.
Mr. Mark Sopworth would never marry her; he
knew on which side his bread was buttered too well
for that ! and if all was true about old Crawley, Mary
Wheeler must go out into some situation, for she
had no rich relations to take her."

So talked Mrs. Barker to Mrs. Morland. In a day
or two she was sitting with Miss Lizzy Sopworth,
and talking about Mr. Morland. "Well, she thanked
God that her husband was a man of business, and not
like Mr. Morland ! But, really, it was a shooking
thing, such a fortune as Mr. Nixon had made ; and
now people said that Morland, though he began with
three or four thousand pounds, was insolvent ! But
he really was never likely to make any business succeed ; he paid no attention to it—he neglected his
business shockingly. Moorson, the druggist, was
making all the same perfumes now. Morland was

a wild, dissipated sort of man they both agreed,
and neglected his wife shamefully; ho never went
with her to church now, and he spent nearly all his
evenings at the Blue Boar, drinking there with commercial gentlemen; they did not believe that Mrs.
Morland was happy—how, indeed, could she be
so? Mrs. Barker had heard hints dropped—but she
hated repeating all that she heard—however, she was
certain that if she had such a husband, she would
read him a pretty lesson! But they should all see
soon what would be the end of all this; Mr. Morland
would get into the Gazette as well as old Crawley, and
then he must take to his travelling again; and if that
did not bring down his wife's pride, they did not know
what would."

The summer wore on, and old Crawley and his
niece, and Mr. and Mrs. Morland, furnished much
material for gossip. It may, perhaps, be imagined,
that, if there were really cause, or only ground for
some of the many and painful things that were
said, the intimacy between Mary Wheeler and her
friend must have become greater than ever, out of
natural interchange of sorrows and mutual sympathy:
but that was not exactly the case; Mary Wheeler
and Mrs. Morland had, of late, met less frequently
than hitherto, and neither one nor the other spoke
much of the sorrow that haunted them. Mrs. Morland, indeed, said nothing, whilst she respected her
young friend's delicacy of feeling too much to pry
into whatever she might choose to conceal. As to Mrs.
Morland, we will look a little nearer into her growing
and unlooked for troubles.

Mrs. Morland had always regarded herself as most

happily married, and had the most intense admiration
and affection for her husband. He was, by many
people, considered as very handsome. He had been
a commercial traveller all his life, and, with his
guinea a day, and his handsome horse and gig, had
lived a gay and easy life; secure of his income, confident of his own cleverness in all that was required
from him, and proud of his character among his commercial brethren, as one of the most respected and
respectable travellers on the road, and a thorough
good fellow into the bargain. What smiling lips and
brightening eyes of buxom landladies and pretty
chambermaids welcomed George Morland, or "the
handsome traveller" as he was called, to all the best
inns in England! What travellers' rooms he set in
a roar with his gay, witty stories! and what reputation had he not gained for his good singing! There
was not a rich tradesman with whom he did business,
that, if his wife had a party, would not invite him as
one of its most honoured guests. Yes, indeed! it was
a merry life, and a life greatly to his taste, which he
had led.

Much as he knew of trade, he had never felt any
inclination for it on his own account; he pitied people,
indeed—let them make what incomes they would—
who were tied down, all their lives, to a counter.
"Free and easy" was his maxim; and just in the
same degree in which he compassionated the home-
bound shopkeeper, did he regard the married man.
He said, and so said all who knew him, that he would
remain a bachelor, and keep true to his sample-bag
to the end of the chapter; but unexpected events
happen, every now and then, to vary the dull routine

of things, and so it was here. Mr. Morland found
himself, without the remotest expectation of such a
thing; heir to a thousand pounds; and then, all at
once—quite as unexpectedly—the desire to be in trade
on his own account took possession of him, and that
more especially, as Mr. Nixon, for whom he had done
business, died just then, and his business was offered
for sale. Amid a host of applicants for the business
he was successful; he purchased it and the stock in
trade, together with all the late Mr. Nixon's recipes,
and thus became patentee of one single perfume, it
was said, by which its original inventor had cleared
some hundreds a year. Morland thought he had a
fine prospect before him; borrowed an additional
thousand pounds, and established himself, as he
thought, for life. No sooner, however, was he in a
house of his own, than he began to think about a
wife; and just as unexpectedly as he had found
himself possessor of a thousand pounds, he discovered
that the niece of a certain distiller in Bristol was in
possession of his heart. They had known one another
for years. It was our own dear Mrs. Morland: he went
over to Bristol, said all kind of noble-seeming things,
as, how he never had thought himself worthy, a poor
traveller as he was, to aspire to her hand; but now—
here, he was with his first good luck—might he but
be thought worthy of her! We know how all
this affair went on: he married her, and brought her
home, as we have seen.

Mrs. Morland, with all her sound judgment, was
the last person in the world to see faults in any one
whom she loved. She almost adored her husband,
and thought him about as near perfection as any

human being could be ; she found excuses for what
any one but herself would have called faults, and
palliated and justified, not to say cheerfully shut her
eyes, wherever her honest reason might have blamed.
A loving true-hearted woman was this, our dear Mrs.
Morland, and even while her neighbours, Mrs. Barker and Lizzy Sopworth, made themselves quite sure,
that a person who loved handsomely to dress and
handsomely to live, as she did, must long ago have
discovered that her husband would never make a
fortune like Mr. Nixon ;—for nothing at all did he
know of distilling, and old Matthew had hinted how
badly things were managed, and that hundreds of
pounds' worth of spirit, and such things, were wasted,
because Mr. Morland no more understood his business than a child ;—whilst all this, and a deal more,
was talked of by her ill-natured neighbours, Mrs.
Morland herself was trying more and more to make
home comfortable and attractive to her "dear George,"
as she always called him.

When people are unprosperous in a worldly point
of view, or even when they are dissatisfied with themselves, it mostly happens that the temper is the moral
barometer which indicates these things. " A prosperous man can afford to be good-tempered," said
Morland, hundreds of times to himself, and not to
himself only, but to his wife also. Thus it was that
the very first acknowledgements which she made to
her husband's disadvantage, were on the score of his
temper. " His temper," she argued, " was not very
good—was not always alike ; but she could not expect
all men to be like her uncle ; he was a man in ten
thousand !" And then, recalling the domestic unhap-

piness of her own home, which, candid as she was,
she attributed more to the faults of her mother than
her father, she resolved to use redoubled efforts that
nothing on her part should be wanting to secure
comfort and affection to their fireside.   The idea
that her husband was inadequate to his business, and
that he was in a fair way to lose not only what was
his own, but what he had borrowed likewise, never
entered her mind.   She feared only that he missed
some accustomed pleasures and indulgences; therefore,
she only the more consulted his tastes, gratified his
whims and fancies, and met him always with affectionate smiles and cheerful words, nor ever breathed
a syllable of the wish which lay nearest to her heart
—that he would spend more of his evenings with her
than with his old friends at the Blue Boar.

Mr. Morland was a man who had a perfect passion
for clothes; his wardrobe was most extraordinary, at
least it seemed so to his wife, who had been accustomed
to her father's painful but necessary economy, and to
her uncle's moderation.   What a number and variety
of great-coats, cloaks, and macintoshes, did she not
find him possessed of!   To say nothing of other
clothes, there was a whole closet-full of trousers; and
waistcoats had he by dozens, satin, and velvet, and
cloth — of every variety of manufacture.   It was necessary, he said, for him to dress well; travelling spoiled
many clothes, and he often got tired of a thing as soon
as it was made; or it went out of fashion, or something or other.   Mrs. Morland thought that, now her
husband did not travel, and lived quite at home, it
would be much better to wear some of the old things
out; but he had different views; he sold half his

wardrobe to a Jew, and then bought a fresh supply. Not a month passed but something or other came home from the tailor's, and Mrs. Morland, who found he would have his way, only smiled.

Midsummer, however, came, and with it Midsummer bills. " My dear George," exclaimed she, opening a long bill from Hawkins, the draper, " do we really owe him five-and-forty pounds ! I have not bought one single thing since the table-linen, and we paid for that at Christmas—nay ! and here it actually is again ? fifteen pounds, as you may remember ; and all the rest is for—" She did not say for what, because it was for his clothes, and she never even hinted that he did wrong.

" And what the devil did you lay out fifteen pounds for table-linen for?" returned he, roused out of the silence into which he had sunk.

" Fifteen pounds !" returned his wife ; " why, my dear George, you surely do not call that much for family table-linen ; and there was none, you know, dearest, when I came. We ought, really, every year to make a little purchase till we had a good stock ; but I am so surprised that this was not paid at Christmas !"

Morland started up, and, without another word, went out, banging the parlour door after him, and the next moment she heard him leave the house. The thought of the unpaid Christmas bill lay most unpleasantly on her mind. It was a dull, sultry evening ; her parlour-windows opened into the Barkers' yard ; there was no fresh air to be had, and she was beginning to think of taking a little solitary walk, when a low tap at the door was heard, and Mary Wheeler

entered. Poor Mary! her eyes, too, were red; she
had been weeping—she, too, was unhappy! All at
once it seemed as if a veil were withdrawn from Mrs.
Morland's mental vision, and human life lay before
her, not steeped in the roseate light of affection, as it
mostly seemed to her cheerful spirit, but dark and
troubled, and full of difficulties and uncertainties
What if she and her husband came to be dissatisfied
with each other—came to live in strife together—to
have secrets and misunderstandings! And it might
be so! There was a deal of unhappiness in this
world; much disunion and bitterness in families—and
if it came to be their case! And with this thought
she suddenly burst into tears; it was what Mary
Wheeler had never seen her do before. *She*, then, had
troubles of her own! Perhaps, indeed, thought Mary,
all those unpleasant things which people say are
true; perhaps Mr. Morland is nearly ruined; perhaps
he is unkind to his wife!—A flood of sympathy
overflowed the kind-hearted girl, and without saying
one word, she laid her head upon her shoulder, and
wept too. She had come to open all her troubles to
her friend; to ask her serious and most friendly
counsel, but this was not the time; nor, of course, did
she solicit the confidence of Mrs. Morland. Very
little indeed was said by either of them. Mary took
out her work as usual, and Mrs. Morland got hers.
Yet, though their conversation was all of common-
places, never did they part before with such friendly
feelings towards each other.

" I 've been devilishly cheated in this cursed concern," said Morland, one day, throwing himself into a
chair, " and I'll commence an action against Nixon's
executors for imposition."

" Has Matthew failed again, then?" asked his wife, for she had long been accustomed to hear of his blunders.

In the fulness of his indignation against Nixon's executors, he told her that Matthew knew nothing; that Nixon, he found, had never let him into his secrets, that he had done everything himself. The processes, he said, he believed to be simple enough ; but that, as he could not make them succeed, he was convinced that something or other had been withheld from him, and he was determined to commence a prosecution.

Mrs. Morland thought that such a step would be the most imprudent in the world, as it would only be publishing that he could not produce articles equal to those of the late Mr. Nixon.

"Do not do so, for Heaven's sake!" said she. " Try again : try again and again, and that with only small proportions, so that, in case of failure, there may not be much loss ; but, above all things, keep from the public the knowledge of any want of success whatever. Try yet again, dearest," said she, kissing him affectionately, "and all will go right!"

Morland tried again, and again ; but things did not go right. Weeks went on ; his temper got more irritable than ever ; and the draper's bill remained unpaid.

Mary Wheeler, one day, brought in the purse which she had made for her brother; it was quite finished, rings and tassels and all, and was handsome enough to contain the gold of an earl.

" How pleased your brother will be with it !" said Mrs. Morland ; "and when does he come ?"

I

Without answering, Mary burst into tears, and Mrs. Morland instantly imagined that her uncle would not allow him to come; she felt almost as much excited as Mary herself: "Oh, do tell me, Mary," she said; "is he not coming?"

"Oh dear! I do not know," said Mary, at length, wiping her eyes; "I never felt in such a state of excitement and anxiety in my life before; for I know that, in the temper my uncle now is and has been for many weeks, he would not let him come if he were now in England. And then, only think! he that has lived all this time in the hope of seeing me, that has been away from his native land so long, to come back and have no home, and everybody else have homes to go to and friends to welcome them! And when there is nobody in this world that can be so dear to another as Ned is to me, not to be allowed to come to see me! I really think it will make me lose my senses."

"He must—he will let him come!" said the hopeful Mrs. Morland.

"Oh," said poor Mary, "what have I not done to get him into good humour, and how frightened have I been to see how the time was going on! To-morrow is the 1st of September, and so as I have wished for the time to come! Now, if it were in my power, I would make it stand still; for, oh, if this time goes by and I do not see him, it may be years before I see him again—if I ever do—for I may die, or he may; or—one does not know what may happen!"

"But, my dear girl," said Mrs. Morland, "you are terrifying yourself about imaginary things; when he really comes, your uncle will be as glad to see him as ou will."

Mary heaved a deep sigh, and then continued : " I have so longed to talk to you, dear Mrs. Morland, but I dislike so much to be always complaining ; and then, for a long time, I thought I ought not to mention many things which made me uneasy ; but you must have heard —everybody has—all the neighbours' servants know it—about my uncle's arrest, and all the terrible rumours there are about him. They say he will be a bankrupt ; I do not know, I am sure, for you know one cannot speak of these things; but I have had many thoughts and questionings with myself of what I ought to do. Heaven knows, that if I could do anything for my uncle, I would ; he has found me a home for many years, and then he let Ned be gratified in the choice of a profession. I feel that I owe him something ; but, oh, Mrs. Morland, indeed, indeed," sobbed she, " my uncle's house is hardly a fit home for a young girl ! Many, many things, more than the world really knows, make me unhappy. I want—indeed I do—a friend to counsel with and to advise me. If Ned were to come, I should tell him all, and ask him what I should do. If my poor unfortunate uncle is bankrupt, or goes to jail, I then must do something. I will take a place in a school ; I will serve in a shop ; I will even be a common servant, for indeed I am not proud : and let me be where I may, I cannot have much more to bear than I have already borne !" Mary wept, and Mrs. Morland, full of sympathy and kindness, forgetting all her own anxieties, began to think that she would persuade her husband to invite Mary's brother to their house, in case Mr. Crawley refused to let him go there.

"Don't be disheartened, dear Mary," said she; "you'll see your brother—I'm sure you will. And then, as to all you say about its being an unfit home for you with your uncle, that I am sure of. We will all three of us—Ned and you and I—consider what is best to be done!" Mary made no answer; and Mrs. Morland began to think of her young friend's future, in which of course, as it always did, mingled the idea of Mr. Mark Sopworth. She began, therefore, quite naturally to speak of the Sopworths.

"Ah! there's another trouble," said Mary. "Lizzy Sopworth is not at all friendly with me now. I don't know how it is, but she has never been quite friendly with me since last Christmas, and if ever her brother shows me the least attention, it is sure to displease her." The last attention, as she frankly confessed, but not without blushes, which he had shown her, was in walking home with her from Sommerton, where they had accidentally met. She did not think, either, that his family were as friendly to her as they used to be; she fancied that they were influenced by all those shocking things respecting her uncle. People used to fancy him rich, and that she would be his heir; but, however that might be, Mr. Mark had been more than commonly friendly to her that evening; they had talked a deal about her brother: she could not help crying, she said; and then he had been so kind—it was impossible for her to say how kind he had been!

Mrs. Morland, as was very natural, spoke of the time when she would be Mrs. Mark Sopworth, and of what a happiness it would be for her to have a house of her own, to invite her brother to. Mary said that she had often thought of these things herself, and that really the prospect of having a home of one's own was enough to make a woman marry, provided she had any respect for a man.

Mrs. Morland thought so too; and then added, that, whatever the family of the Sopworths might feel regarding her, she was quite convinced that Mark was excessively in love with her; and she felt sure, that if anything really unfortunate happened to Mr. Crawley, Mary would have a home provided for her, without the necessity either of serving in a shop or going into a school.

Blessed are those friends and counsellors who think as we do! Mary was happier that night, as she laid her head on her pillow, than she had been for months.

CHAPTER VII.

A TURN IN THE TIDE.

"I'LL never stir another stroke in this cursed business!" said Morland, bursting into the parlour one of the next days—"never, as long as I live; and the devil may do his worst with it!" ♦

Mrs. Morland, as she had done many a time before, tried to pacify and soothe; and hoped and felt sure that all would be right, and that her husband would succeed if he would only persevere. It was such a thing, she said, to be disheartened, and to give anything up in despair! She should never doubt succeeding herself, if she were to try; and she was quite

sure, that if he would only think so, he would succeed too. Oh, it was absurd to think of anything else!
"If I could only have been contented to be as I
was!" exclaimed he, deaf to the voice of the charmer,
—"with a guinea a day, and no responsibility, instead
of paying a thousand pounds for what is not worth a
thousand pence, and then to have borrowed money
besides! Heavens! it makes me mad."

His wife still talked cheerfully, still tried to
make him take a more hopeful view of things—and,
above all, to have confidence in himself.

"I am next door to a beggar!" said he, looking
fiercely at her; for all that she said, in the honest
belief of her soul, of his abilities for business and
ultimate success, seemed to him bitter irony. "In
half a year—ay, in three months—I shall be a bankrupt. I hate the whole concern, and that's the long
and short of it; and I wish the devil had it!" And
then, in a sort of desperation, which was not without
a tinge of malice, he brought out his books to show
her how his affairs really stood, and to prove to her,
he said, what a fool she was to talk of ultimate
success, and such stuff. Melancholy indeed was it to
see large, heavily-bound ledgers, which seemed calcu-
lated for a business whose proud returns should be ten
thousand a year; containing, at their very outset, a
balance of loss—loss—loss! She thought to herself,
that her husband did well indeed to keep them under
lock and key; for what would Barker or Sopworth
say, could they surmise even of such things!

It was an astounding discovery—one for which she
was not prepared; and she sate with her head resting
on her hand in deep thought, from which she was

roused by her husband's words. He would sell, he said, his business for what he could get for it, and take again to his commercial travelling—from the salary for which he must contrive to allow her a hundred a year, or something like that. It was a good thing, he said, that they had no family; she and a servant could live very well on that, for nobody would expect much show from a bankrupt's wife.

This was the cruellest blow that could have fallen on poor Mrs. Morland; she could not at first believe that her husband really meant what he said. To live separated from him—him whom she loved so ardently, was to her inconceivable; she would rather live on bread-and-water with him, than like a queen without him; his affection for her must indeed be very different to hers, if he could mean what he said. But then, that that husband should be a bankrupt! Oh, heavens! with all her upright notions of trade and tradesmen, as derived from the knowledge of her uncle, that was worse even than all the rest; for, to be a bankrupt was to her mind the height and depth of disgrace! To have begun with two thousand pounds, and in two years not to be able to pay more than three shillings in the pound, as her husband's books seemed to prove, what a disgraceful thing it was! She thought of Hawkins's unpaid bill; she thought of many another unpaid bill; and the prospect seemed most appalling!

But Mrs. Morland—bless her noble spirit! was not a woman to sink down tamely under misfortune, especially when that misfortune was of a kind to leave a stain on the fair fame of her husband. Her first thought and hope was that she would encourage him to help himself out of his difficulties; her second, and more mature one, was, that she herself would endeavour to help him.

" George, dearest," said she to him one day, soon after these terrible things had come to her knowledge, "two things are certain,—our affairs are desperate, and they must be mended. Let *me* undertake the preparation of the perfumes. I am no fine lady, thank God ! I care not what this person or that says about anything I do, so that we can only keep a good name ! Oh, George," continued she, " you know not what difficulties I have conquered in my life, and if I were to tell you, you would perhaps think nothing of them ; but they have given me confidence in myself ; and self-reliance, with judgment, will overcome great difficulties ! Yes, you may smile," said she, " but a drowning man will catch at a straw ; here, then, see the straw which I hold out to you, and which, please God to prosper me, shall not prove a straw, but a good sound bridge to carry you over !"

We need not go through all the pros and cons in the affair. Like the widow in the gospel, in the end she carried her point. Her husband consented—but with an ill-grace, we must confess—that she should make the attempt ; he all the while assuring her that she was a fool, and would only end by making the three shillings in the pound, which the creditors might now receive, three halfpence ; but it did not matter, he said ; she should be a nine days' wonder, any how !

Poor Mrs. Morland ! A great responsibility seemed laid upon her, as the next day she set about her work in good earnest. Her husband, however, prepared his portmanteau, and set out, as he said, on an absence of a week. She never inquired where he was going, nor did he seem inclined to tell her ; but, just at that time, she could not help finding his absence a great relief.

It was one of the most delicate and renowned of Nixon's perfumes on which Mrs. Morland made her first attempt. She found the process most clearly laid down by Nixon in his private book, and the process seemed easy and simple ; it only required precision and strict attention. Her husband had failed every time—if she could accomplish that, she need despair of none. She scarcely breathed as the work went on ; with her watch in her hand, she saw it distilling drop by drop ; if it succeeded, it was like so much pure gold : if she failed, what then ?—Why she would try again, and again !

"Thank God! thank God!" exclaimed she, examining the ethereal liquid, which she had prepared, and inhaling its most refined odour ; "this must be right."

The postman brought in a letter—it was from her husband in London. He wrote to say, that he was in treaty to dispose of his business, and had already a prospect of re-engagement with the old firm for which he had formerly travelled. He should not be back, he said, for a fortnight, and he intended that she should remove to London, which would be a much more agreeable home for her than a gossiping place like W— would be, after the disagreeables which were inevitable. He asked, he said, eight hundred pounds for his business, but would be quite willing to take five for it. In a postscript he added that it was not the least use in the world her endeavouring to turn him ; his mind was quite made up, and he should close the bargain as soon as possible.

All the pleasure of success was damped by this letter ; she wrote instantly to her husband to inform him of her success, and to beseech of him not to dispose of a business which was worth ten times the money he asked for it.

The letter was despatched ; and as she sat in the evening, pondering almost gloomily on the unfortunate concurrence of circumstances, Becky came in, and said that Miss Wheeler wanted to see her. "Let her come, certainly," said she ; and Mary Wheeler entered. Both of them looked out of spirits, and for some time scarcely anything was said.

"You have heard, of course," said Mrs. Morland, at length, "what everybody is saying about us." Mary confessed that she had ; people were so surprised, she said ; it seemed to make her uncle's affairs sink into insignificance, and she could never herself express how grieved she was.

"Please God !" said Mrs. Morland, "all may be better before long ; but this is a blow I was very little prepared for," added she, unable to avoid weeping. Mary so seldom saw her weep, and weeping too on her own account, that there was something inexpressibly affecting to her in it ; she clasped her arms round her neck like a loving child, and while she kissed her tenderly, wept too, for sincerest sympathy.

"But," said Mrs. Morland, rousing up at length, "I want to know, Mary, whether your brother is coming ?"

The question turned poor Mary's thoughts at once into their old channel ; she grew quite pale, and,

without replying, fixed her eyes on Mrs. Morland,
with a look almost of despair, that went to her
very soul. " Poor dear child !" said she ; and Mary,
opening her little black silk bag, took thence a letter,
which she put into her hand. It was a letter from
Ned himself, dated "off Gravesend" but a few days
before ; a joyful, affectionate letter, full of the anti-
cipation of meeting. Whilst Mrs. Morland read it,
Mary sate with her eyes fixed upon her, almost
breathless ; and, when she had finished, clasped her
hands, and burst into a passion of tears.

" And do you really mean to say that your brother
is not coming ?" asked she.

" He is not coming," returned Mary, in a mcurn-
ful voice ; " my uncle has utterly forbidden it. I
went down on my knees," said she, " to him yesterday,—I besought him with prayers and tears, but it
was no use ; nothing but despair, which drove me
almost frantic, would have made me venture so far ;
and if I had been begging for my life, I could not
have prayed more earnestly, but it was no use ;—he
says he cannot afford it ! Oh, what a miserable
thing it is to be poor !" exclaimed she. " If I could
only in any way raise five pounds, that he might
come ! but all the money that ever I could save, I
laid out for him in a silk handkerchief, and that
miserable purse, which I thought I should have such
pleasure in giving him !"

Mrs. Morland thought of her own former wishes to
invite Mary's brother to their house, in case his uncle
refused ; and she sighed deeply, remembering, alas
her own inability to do so.

" Perhaps," said Mary, after a few seconds, during

which Mrs. Morland made no remark, "you think
that, in the present state of my uncle's affairs, I ought
not to have urged him to spend even one penny on
me or Ned, and that I am unreasonable ever to think
of such a thing;—perhaps I am : but this I know
that I feel as if I could not live without seeing him,
and I think it is only natural that I should feel so,
especially when I know that he is in England, and
that he has no particular friends in London, and that
he wants to see me so much. And, oh," said she,
speaking almost wildly, "there are so many, so very
many things on which I want his counsel ; he always
seemed so much older in judgment than I ; and ho
has travelled so far, and seen so much, that I am sure
he could advise me for the best !"

Mrs. Morland thought to herself that a youth who
had lived so much at sea, very probably had had
really far less experience in life than the poor girl
herself, but she did not say so ; and Mary added,
"There are many things on which I wanted to open
my heart to him, and to know his opinion."

Mrs. Morland readily imagined what these were.
The state of her affections, probably, was as little
happy as her prospects in life, for she herself had
often thought, though she had never said so to Mary,
that if Mark Sopworth really had no matrimonial
intentions towards her, he was trifling very cruelly,
not to say shamefully, with her feelings ; and if he
had, now was the time of all others to come forward
—now when she so deeply needed true friends and a
home.

"I don't wonder, dear Mary," said she, "at your
wanting to see your brother; it is no more than

natural, and I wish to Heaven you could !" And then she told her what had been her intentions, and what nothing but their own misfortunes would have prevented her from doing. Mary threw her arms again round her neck, and kissed her tenderly, for this proof of intended kindness touched her beyond words. " I know how good and generous you are," said she ; " and if it had not been for you, what would have become of me ? And I would, and should," added she, " have asked your advice long ago, but I knew that you had troubles and anxieties of your own ; and a hoped that Ned would come !'"

Days went on, and many a wild scheme had poor Mary to procure means to enable her brother to come to W—. His letters, though intended to reconcile her to their mutual disappointment, almost broke her heart ; and when at length she received from him a packet of beautiful Indian trifles, which he found an opportunity of sending to her free of cost, she was almost beside herself. " If I could only borrow five pounds," thought she, " I would go into service, and never rest till it was paid back again ;" and had it not been that Mrs. Morland was unfortunate herself, she would have asked it from her. She thought of Miss Harris ; but, oh, no ! Miss Harris would do nothing which seemed counter to Mr. Crawley's wishes. She thought of Mark Sopworth. Heaven help her, poor girl ! she had thought of him all the time ; but though she told Lizzy Sopworth of her distress, Lizzy's sympathy was cold, for she and Barbara Pocklington were going to the Assize ball, and had neither time nor thought to spend on anybody's troubles. Mary saw Mark himself—met him in the street, and actually stopped him—such a thing as she had never done before, to tell him her distress. He turned back with her, and walked, not homeward, but into the pleasant fields below the town. He was sympathisingly kind, more than as a friend, almost as a lover; but yet— oh yes, a woman's heart is sensitive as life itself,—it was not, after all, quite that generous, self-forgetting, all-sacrificing kindness, which is the true characteristic of true love! She was more than ever depressed as she sate down in her own chamber, after her return, not knowing that Barbara Pocklington, who had seen them together, was sitting also in her chamber, a prey to the fiend jealousy.

The day after Mrs. Morland received her husband's letter, she wrote to her uncle, begging him to come to her immediately. He came; and the very day he came, Morland wrote again to his wife, but in wretched spirits; he thought nothing at all of her success, but was greatly disturbed that the bargain was all off about disposing of his business. There was a rumour abroad, he said, to his disadvantage; and everywhere people were imitating Nixon's perfumes. Nobody would purchase the concern, because the patent was so invaded. He talked of prosecution, and then cursed his poverty. There never was such a miserable letter written before!

By the time Mrs. Morland's uncle came, she had worked up all the stock which her husband had left, and had re-supplied the warehouse with sundry dozens of whatever articles were most in demand; and what was yet more to the purpose was, that whatever she had prepared was finer almost than that which had been made by the original inventor. " I am lucky! God be thanked; I am indeed lucky!" said dear Mrs. Morland, with tears in her eyes, at the very moment when her uncle's rap at the door startled her.

We tell nothing of the meeting of uncle and niece; we merely say, that he was perfectly satisfied of her success, and of her ability to conduct the business; that he gave her the most cordial encouragement and approbation, and consented to become nominally the purchaser of the business, for five hundred pounds, which he would advance immediately, to enable her, and, in fact, on condition of her becoming joint conductor and manager of the concern. All was happily and satisfactorily arranged; and while not only the Barkers and the Sopworths, but the whole neighbourhood were, not whispering of the Morland's embarrassment, but almost shouting it aloud, Mrs. Morland wrote a joyful letter to her husband.

" Return, dearest," said she, " for things are not so bad but that they will readily be repaired. Your business has begun already to flourish. I hoped, in marrying you, to bring a blessing into your house; of money, Heaven knows I brought but little, but that is of less consequence, if I can help you to acquire it.

" But, in order that I may make myself intelligible to you, I must tell you, that, by the blessing of Heaven, I have entirely and altogether succeeded in making and distilling those particular perfumes on which you set most value. My uncle, for whom I sent, and on whose judgment I know you too set a high value, has been here. He entirely approves of all that I have done, and testifies to my success. He will advance us the necessary money to go on with, so that there is no fear of your becoming bankrupt. Gracious Heaven!

the idea of your being so disgraced would almost drive me mad! I am happy, George—supremely happy, in feeling myself to be the means of helping you, and keeping your name free from stain.   ·

"Thank God! we may now live together ; for, to tell you the truth, nothing in this world, excepting disgrace itself, is so bitter as to be separated from you. Come home then, dearest, as soon as you can, and give up the horrid idea of travelling, which, in point of respectability, is nothing to compare to a clever, flourishing tradesman, who is his own master, and whose profits are all for himself. I am proud of being a tradesman's wife, and, above all, of being yours ! Come back, then, to your own wife, and make her perfectly happy, by saying, ' Well done, good and faithful servant !' Yes, George, I say come back, and your wife will be your helper—your helpmate, as the Creator from the first intended all wives to be."

Morland read the letter, and came home, not so much because his wife wished it, as because he had completed his own arrangements, signed and sealed his agreement with Willet and Skeggs, to become once more their commercial traveller, and was now at liberty to look after his own brangled affairs, and to make an end one way or another of that " cursed business," as he still continued to call it. He read his wife's letter, and did her the justice to say that there was not in this world a better wife than his, and that it was a pity she had ever married an unfortunate dog like himself ; but as to having any faith in her distilling and perfume-compounding, he had none ; and as to the five hundred which the uncle had lent, why, if he chose to purchase the business, and let his niece manage it for him, that was another thing : but as to borrowing the money, with interest to pay on it, that he would never consent to ; and he did not exactly like that the state of his affairs, without his own knowledge, should have been laid open to anybody, and more especially to a precise, clever man of business like his wife's uncle, who looked on insolvency as worse than leprosy.

So thought Morland ; and, so thinking, came home. The uncle was gone when he arrived, and his wife was busy again distilling, and working down in the little laboratory with as much zeal as ever Nixon had worked there before her. Her husband's laugh, as he entered unperceived, and stole softly behind her, made her first aware of his presence. She threw her arms round his neck, and kissed his lips, his cheeks, and his forehead ;—the joyful affection of his wife made him for the moment unspeakably happy.

"And now," said she, putting the key of the laboratory into her pocket, " before you eat or drink, you shall see the grain of mustard-seed which I have sown for our future prosperity."

Morland saw what his wife had done ; and, after examination, proved to him how well she had done it too : yet, for all this—and we write it with regret— he gave her but very measured commendation. He did not say, as he ought to have done, and as in the bottom of his heart he felt all the time, that she, in having succeeded where he had failed, had become his good angel, and had saved him from disgrace and ruin ; and beyond that, that she must be regarded as the agent of their future prosperity.

Nothing of this sort did Mr. Morland say, but
K 2

talked very coolly. He hoped things would turn out well; hoped she might ultimately succeed, but did not feel at all sure; the things which she had prepared might or might not be right, time would prove —and time would prove, too, whether her present success was not rather accident than anything else! He could not say, for his part; and so on.

Buoyant-hearted as Mrs. Morland naturally was, she could not help confessing that it was a little discouraging to hear him talk so ; her uncle had spoken very differently ; she was sorry that her husband was not as well pleased as she had hoped he would be. But, after all, added she, what did it matter? the main thing was accomplished,—the business would succeed ; he would give her all the credit she deserved as soon as the money began to come in ; and, in the meantime, she should have him with her, to make happy and to love !

Alas ! the coolness with which he had regarded all her good works gave not half the pain which she endured a few days afterwards, on finding from him, that on the 23d of December he must be in London, in order to prepare for entering on his new situation with the commencement of the year! He said she should have the management of the business for the next twelve months, but that if there were loss, it must stand against her uncle's name ; he would keep to the bargain she had made with him,—the five hundred pounds was the purchase-money of the concern. He washed his hands of the affair, he said, and would be responsible for no further loss ; and if, at the end of the twelve months, it did not answer, the uncle must make his best of it, and she must go to

London. He himself, he said, had found a friend, too, who had advanced him five hundred pounds; he would settle with all his creditors, and thus leave her and her uncle a fair field to start upon.

Mr. Morland went, as he said he should, on the 23d of December, but not, however, before he had compensated to his wife for his former coldness to her. The truth was, he loved her better than he ever fancied he could love a wife; and all the noble efforts she had made to save him from ruin touched his heart deeply.

"I cannot think," said he to himself, as he was putting up a case of those exquisite perfumes, which she had prepared with such singular success, as a sample of what he was able to supply to Nixon's old customers, "I cannot think," mused he, "how a worthless, wretched dog like me, who cannot manage to keep a good business from bankruptcy, ever came to get such a good wife!"

He rolled up the black morocco sample-case, and went on thinking of his wife, and how much handsomer she really was, and how vastly superior every way to all those handsome clever landladies who, at so many an inn which he had been accustomed to frequent, used to be his admiration.

"Hang it!" thought he to himself, as he put the sample-case into his carpet-bag, "the warmest welcome is not always at an inn. I'm spoiled for travelling now, I'm afraid; and with such a wife it's no wonder; and yet I can't think how ever I had the impudence to ask her to have me; however, I'll save something out of my guinea a-day, as sure as my name is Morland; and, instead of buying so many clothes for myself, I'll now and then buy something for her!"

CHAPTER VIII.

IT was Christmas Day—a cold, wet, and miserable Christmas Day ; and Mrs. Morland, who had, spite of the weather, been to church—for when the heart is sad, it is naturally disposed to communion with its Maker, sate late in the evening, as she had sate for the greatest part of the afternoon, alone and sunk in deep thought, by her own fireside.   She had been taking a review of her past life, and looking forward to the future, and had been covenanting with herself and with God for the conscientious and zealous and unwavering fulfilment of all the requirings of her duty, let them be what they might.   Her thoughts were serious, but not desponding ; and, like a light, at once cheering and warm, there lived about her heart the remembrance of her husband's parting words.   Let us see what they were as she at that moment recalled them to her mind—" God bless you, Ellen, and let me tell you what I think of myself.   I ought to be torn with wild horses for not making you a better husband.   I don't know how it is, but I never thought what sort of husband you deserved till of late ; but I shall be an altered man, Ellen, and all the good that comes to us is owing to you !   I can't think how in the world you came to marry me ; but I'll make you a good husband yet, never fear ! and I'll make you amends one way or another, that I will !   And so,

God bless you, Ellen; and take care of yourself, for my sake; but don't cry now, Ellen! and I shall write to you every Sunday. I am no great church-goer, as you know, but love to one's wife—and such a wife as you—is every bit as good as religion; and whenever I think of you I shall bless God, and that is religion, too! But I must go, or I shall cry myself; and a big fellow like me looks such a fool crying! So, good-bye!" And as he went out of the house he blew his nose very loudly, which his wife never failed to remember also, for it was a sign that, big fellow as he was, he could not help crying too.

Mrs. Morland sate by her fire quite alone; and while she was thus sitting, the Barkers, and the Pocklingtons, and dozens of people beside—all those, in fact, who had met at the Sopworths', of Sommerton, twelve months before, with the exception of the Morlands and old Crawley and his niece, met there again for another Christmas party. Again there was the same good dinner; the same swinging mistletoe, the same games, and the same merriment; but at dinner and supper, and even in the midst of all the mirth, two most interesting topics occupied every one; and they were the ruin of Mr. Crawley and the embarrassment of Mr. Morland. According to them, Crawley was a bankrupt not worth a penny in the pound; and if Morland could pay half-a-crown, that was the outside.

" And what will become of Miss Wheeler?" asked some one.

" What will young Sopworth do?" or, " Was it only a flirtation?" asked many another; and to these last questions the very next moment seemed to give

answer, in what they beheld before them. Barbara
Pocklington was telling fortunes with cards; and
Mark Sopworth, who was leaning over the back of
her chair, kept whispering in her ear. Nobody heard
exactly what he whispered, but Barbara looked more
than pleased ; and somebody who saw it declared,
afterwards, that he not only whispered into her ear,
but that he impressed a kiss upon her cheek.

"Oh yes," said everybody, "the Pocklingtons
have very good fortunes ; old Mr. Pocklington farms
on his own land, and Mr. Mark Sopworth might do
a deal worse than marry the handsome Barbara!"

Nobody whatever that Christmas day seemed to
think that there was the least chance of Mary
Wheeler becoming Mrs. Mark Sopworth. Then,
as for Mrs. Morland! Well! it was the oddest
thing in the world that Morland should take to his
travelling again; and his wife take upon herself the
management of a half-ruined concern like that! It
was very odd indeed! for somebody had said that
Mrs. Morland really could manage the distilling and
all that, better even than her husband; but it was
not at all likely, for how could she read Latin? And
yet, old Matthew said she did manage, one way or
another, and went on, for all the world, just as Mr.
Nixon used to do. It was a very odd thing, they
said, and more especially as everybody expected to
find Morland's name in the Gazette ; but all his
town bills were paid, and that did not much look like
bankruptcy ; but, at all events, there was an end of
her gentility. They wondered now whether she
would go out in all her fine satins and velvets ; they
should not, they were sure, if they were in her place,

seeing she was not much better than a bankrupt's wife, and a deserted wife into the bargain.

Somebody said, that, as to dressing, she dressed every bit as well as ever; they had seen her at the parish-church that morning, and she was dressed ever so grand! But, however, this time next year would show what would be the end of all this! Yes, said everybody, they should see this time next year!

Whilst people were thus talking of her, she was sitting, as we have seen, by her own fireside, thinking of her husband and his parting words. The sleety rain drove against the window; the wind howled down the chimney, and all at once, the dismal weather without forced itself, as it were, upon her heart. She thought of poor wanderers and homeless people; of wretched mothers, and little children, night-travellers on the tops of coaches; she thought of her husband—great-coated, yet cold—who, on many a night like this, would be driving on in an open gig, over wide windy moors, towards some dreary great town, where he had no friends, and only a noisy inn for his home; and as she thought, life seemed a sad and painful chapter of miseries. She stirred up the fire, which was burning black, to cheer away the despondency which seemed creeping over her, and just at that moment, Becky burst into the room, and at once diverted her thoughts and demanded her attention.

'Only think!" exclaimed she, "of that old brute at the end of the yard! He has turned out that poor thing on a night like this into the driving rain, with nothing but a shawl over her head; and she his own flesh and blood, as one may say!"

"Mary Wheeler turned out on a night like this!"

said Mrs. Morland. " Fetch her in ! " exclaimed she, rushing at once to the door. Becky opened the front door, and the wild wind which met them almost took away their breath.

Mrs. Morland looked out, but the night was pitch-dark. Sopworth's back-shop windows, as it was Christmas-day, were all closed, and not a glimmer of light shone in heaven or on earth, and the driving rain beat into her face.

" Oh, you can't go out ! " said Becky ; " she stands, poor thing, in the shed below Sopworth's kitchen, by her uncle's door ; but the rain drives through the broken roof, and she will be wet to the skin ! "

" Fetch her in ! fetch her in ! for Heaven's sake ! " said Mrs. Morland, hastening back to the parlour, and piling up a good fire ; whilst the kind-hearted Becky, almost as full of pity as her mistress, threw her apron over her head, and went out into the storm.

Mary came in very pale and wet, and looking ill, and very wretched. Her hair, which was dripping with rain, hung forlornly about her face ; there was something so wild and melancholy in her appearance, that Mrs. Morland was almost frightened.

" Why did you not come at once to me ! " said she, somewhat reproachfully ; " you ought to have known that I should stand your friend ! "

" It is a miserable thing to have no home," returned the poor girl ; " and I have been so wretched, that I cared not what became of me. I knew," continued she, " how good, how inexpressibly good you were ; but it is possible to be miserable even beyond caring for oneself ! "

"You should not say so! You should not think
so!" said Mrs. Morland. "God gives us friends,
Mary, that they may help us; he makes our friends
the instruments of his mercy."

"I have had dreadful thoughts—dreadful tempta-
tions this night," at length she said; "but thank God
the worst is over now. I thought of Ned—and I
thought of you, dear Mrs. Morland, and I prayed to
be able to resist temptation, and strength was given
me for it. I was coming to ask you for present
shelter, and for counsel—for, God help me, I need a
friend!—when Becky came to me!"

Like the tenderest of mothers or sisters, Mrs. Morland took her into her own warm chamber, and laid
her in her own bed, comforting her, and encouraging
her to open her whole heart, and make her troubles
light by revealing them. But it would not have
been possible to make her troubles light, nor was it
possible either for her, in the state of mind she then
was, to have revealed them all. But though the kind
Mrs. Morland only at that time knew Mary's troubles
in part, we can tell something of them to the reader.

Mr. Crawley, who had lived for weeks under the
hourly fear of arrest, poured the whole rigour of his
tyrannical temper on his unhappy niece. He was at
length bent upon sending her, or rather conveying
her to London, to an acquaintance of his of very
questionable character, with whom he promised himself, as well as her, a comfortable home. She refused;
and at length, wrought up to passion, which knew no
bounds, and was terrible to witness, he had struck
her, entered her chamber, locked up her few possessions, taken the key, and, throwing to her a

woollen shawl, had turned her out pennyless into
the wild night. Mary described somewhat of her
feelings at that time; she stood, she knew not how
long, before the door in the open rain and wind,
without one definite thought, but of utter wretched-
ness; the world, she said, seemed so wide; but she
had no home in it, and as it seemed, no hope. She
thought of her brother; but the wind howled round
her, and the thought of shipwreck and misery by
sea fell on her soul like death. A kind of dark foreboding came over her, that she should never see him
again, for that he was lost; and a strong wish to die
took possession of her. In that dark moment, too,
she thought of Mark Sopworth, and then came back
the bitter thought which had hung about her all the
day, nay, which had haunted her for many days,
that he and his sister were at Summerton; that it
was Christmas-day; that the party which had met
there the year before, was there again—yet, that
she had not even been invited, was perhaps forgotten
by them. She was of no consequence to them; they
could rejoice without her; they could be gay, even
while the bitterness, as of death, was on her soul.
She thought of Barbara Pocklington—and the miserable feeling of jealousy stung her heart almost to
madness. Heaven forgive her! for she loved truly,
and could not have wounded, even in thought, the
heart she loved! Whilst she was thus suffering
from the intensest torture which the soul can experience, a simple, and otherwise almost ridiculous
circumstance occurred, which only yet more har-
rowed her excited feelings: this was the conversation of two servants—Ann at the Sopworths, and

the Barkers' Sarah. They came into the back-kitchen, near which poor Mary was standing, and while Ann cleaned a saucepan, in which she was intending to mull some wine, Sarah held the candle, and thus they continued the conversation, which seemed to have commenced before.

"Bless me!" said the Barkers' Sarah, "marry her! never! for all she's as fond of him as ever can be! I heard our missis say so myself! Miss Barbara," continued she, "will have two thousand pounds on her wedding-day."

"Which do you think the handsomest?" asked Ann.

"Miss Barbara," returned Sarah; "she has so much more colour. Miss Wheeler is the genteelest, may be: but I wouldn't give a fig for gentility."

"Yes, she is very handsome," said Ann: "she is a deal with our folks now-a-days; and it was very pretty of her to give me the lace for my cap."

"The Pocklingtons give a dance on New Year's Eve," said Sarah, "and our folks go, of course."

"And ours too," said Ann; "master has got a new coat to go in. Oh, it will be a match, as sure as I'm alive; and yet, I used to think he was very fond of Miss Wheeler."

"It was she as was so fond of him," said Sarah; and with these words, the saucepan being sufficiently cleaned, the two returned to the kitchen, leaving poor Mary heart-sick, and doubly wretched.

The very servants talked of her love for him. Heaven help us! how very little can any heart bear to have the naked truth rudely presented to it! Shame and humiliation seemed at once to crush her

to the earth, and make her utterly despise herself.
She thought of self-destruction, and, almost frantic,
rushed into the shed, where she sat for an hour or
more, and where Becky, going for fuel, had seen her.

Better thoughts at length came over her. She
recalled the memory of her parents; she thought of
her beloved brother, and of Mrs. Morland, who had
always been so steadily kind to her. Tears of affection
and tenderness gushed from her eyes; she sank on
her knees, and prayed for strength and resignation,
and then, calmer, if not more hopeful in spirit, rose
up, determined to sin neither against God nor man,
but to ask protection and advice from Mrs. Morland,
whom, it seemed to her at that moment, was the
friend purposely designed by Heaven to help her.

Nothing, however, could Mrs. Morland advise for
the present ; and nothing definite could be done, for
the immediate consequence of Mary's excitement and
exposure to the weather was violent fever, which, for
a considerable time, endangered even her life.

Mr. Crawley was arrested, and without the power
of finding bail ; the creditors took possession of all his
effects, and he himself was removed to prison. Mary
was unconscious of all that was going on around her ;
but Mrs. Morland, ever watchful, and ever thoughtful, interfered with the creditors, and saved for her
her few possessions, the keys of which Mr. Crawley
obstinately refused to give up to any one, but kept
with him in his waistcoat pocket, even in his prison.

The Pocklingtons gave their dance on New Year's
Eve, to which, as a matter of course, the Sopworths
went—Mr. Mark in his new coat, made purposely for
the occasion, as his servant still persisted in saying.

And, again, what a fertile topic of conversation was old Crawley and his affairs! his cruelty to his niece; her illness, and Mrs. Morland's kindness to her;—it was quite a God-send to the party.

" Well, and what will become of poor Miss Wheeler?" asked many a one. She must go out somewhere, everybody agreed; perhaps into a shop, or perhaps into a school, or perhaps she would live altogether with Mrs. Morland, now that Mrs. Morland lived alone, and maintain herself with her needle. Everybody pitied her, and many a one kept their eye fixed, while they talked of her, on Mark Sopworth, to see how he looked; but Mark was aware of that, and though all declared that he looked out of spirits, he either was gay, or assumed purposely an air of gaiety.

Everybody said that they had never seen Barbara look so handsome before; and Barbara devoted herself that night, as everybody said, to fascinate young Sopworth; but as for that, all the Pocklington family overwhelmed him, and his whole connexions, with civilities.

" Oh, it will be a match, as sure as I am alive!" whispered many a one.

One person had heard old Pocklington and young Sopworth talking about somebody purchasing the lease of Crawley's premises from the creditors. Another said it was young Sopworth who was going to purchase; he had said he was intending to live in old Crawley's house, and should turn his own sitting-room into a warehouse. There was, too, a deal of talk on family affairs, between the two mothers. Mrs. Pocklington took Mrs. Sopworth into her bed-

room, where there was a fire, and there they two sat
talking quite confidentially together for more than an
hour.   Nobody had the slightest doubt but that the
marriage of these two young people had become quite
a family affair.

That evening, Mary's life was despaired of; and
Mrs. Morland thought much less of the letter she had
received that day from her husband, though it was
the first he had written since his departure, than she
did of her young friend, who lay insensible on
her bed.

She sat on one side the bed, and Dr. Wentworth,
the physician whom she had called in, sat on the
other.   He showed the warmest interest for his
patient; and no wonder, for she was young and
lovely, and Dr. Wentworth was one of the very best
and kindest of men, whom all loved, but more especially the poor.   He was unmarried, and perhaps five-
and-thirty, and lived with a respectable old housekeeper, and a good establishment of servants, in one
of the best houses of the town.   Mrs. Morland had
known him only by character, till she called him in
to her young inmate; but they very soon became
intimate as old friends.   He often prolonged his
visits to half an hour, or rather so arranged his visit
that he could stay thus long with them.   He had
done so on this occasion; and they two had talked over
the virtues, the sorrows, and the desolate prospects of
the young sufferer before them, till their hearts
seemed overflowing with Christian love and sympathy.
"I shall send my housekeeper to sit up with her to-
night," said he, rising to take his leave; "we must
not make unreasonable demands on you, Mrs. Mor-

land; to-morrow night you shall again sit up with
her—to-night you must sleep."

Dr. Wentworth's housekeeper came, the very per-
sonification of benevolence, cleanliness, and kindness.
It was a real comfort to see her in the chamber;
and, leaving Mary in her care, Mrs. Morland lay
down for a few hours in the next room.

Mary was no better the next day, nor for the three
days following. Lizzy Sopworth stayed at the Pocklingtons' for a week, and Mark, when he returned
home, on the third day of the New Year, was greeted
with the news, that it was doubtful whether Mary
would live through the day. If faith could be put
in the countenance of man, he was not only surprised,
but greatly distressed; if he never had loved her
before, he felt as if he really loved her then; and the
recollection of many things which had occurred since
this last Christmas-day, since Barbara Pocklington
and he had been so much together, rose up in his
mind like accusing spirits.

Like many another man, Mark Sopworth was
infirm of purpose; the present wind, from whatever
point it might blow, carried him before it. He had
been hurried on, as it then seemed to him, farther
than he ever intended with Barbara Pocklington;
he really loved Mary Wheeler, and he knew it now,
though he had never felt quite sure of it before! So
argued he for the first moment, and gave way to a
despondency of feeling which indicated itself in his
countenance, and gave every one of his shopmen a
something to talk about.

It is true, thought he to himself in the course of
the day, that no positive declaration and proposal has

been made to Barbara Pocklington; but it was vain to endeavour to persuade himself that it had not been implied. He had gone no farther with her, nor indeed so far, as with Mary Wheeler; but then, Barbara, unlike poor Mary, had friends to stand by her—brothers, and father, and mother, and sisters; and then, there were his own family—father, and mother, and sister, too, who all would expect this from him; what a host they were! and if he did not fear to disappoint any hopes he had excited in Barbara herself, he *did* fear all this combined force of her friends. If it were not for all these people, thought Mark, I would give up Barbara at once, for I love Mary a thousand times better! And then he thought of her death: and how if she died—what then? he should be quite free to marry Barbara, if he then liked; but, oh no! if Mary died he never would marry—at least, not for many years; it was a beautiful thing to love truly! But he hoped, above all things, that she would not die; for if she died, he never should be happy again!

Mark was extremely glad that his sister was not at home, for if she had, he never could have let her see his feelings; and he never should have ventured to go, as he now would, as soon as ever it was dusk, and ring softly at Mrs. Morland's door, and learn something himself about the poor girl.

Mrs. Morland, who never doubted but that Mark Sopworth really and truly loved, thought it the most natural thing in the world that he should look pale and ill, and that he should be almost too much agitated to speak; so she talked to him in the most kind and friendly manner; told him how ill poor

Mary was, but fearing to distress him too much, gave him hope, and said that she really believed she would get better; and then she began to say how good and amiable she was, and how sure she was that everybody who loved her would come forward and show their regard; that she was so pleased he had been, for she knew what he must be suffering in his own mind; and that she was sure Mary might depend upon her friends. Oh, she was so very good and charming! said she in her enthusiasm, offering her hand, as if in congratulation to Mark; and he might depend upon it she would take all the care of her that was possible, for she knew very well what his feelings must be!

Mrs. Morland's words made him very uncomfortable, strange as it may seem, for he was not quite prepared for anybody else thinking he ought to marry her, or that he was in love with her.' Nevertheless, as Lizzy was not at home, he went in most evenings, when it was dusk; and, though he never again allowed Mrs. Morland time for any particular conversation with him, he only strengthened her belief by this attention, and kept alive his own interest so strongly, that he almost came to the heroic determination that he would marry her when she got better, spite of everybody.

A week went on, and Mary was pronounced quite out of danger. Dr. Wentworth, who had come twice a day, came now but once; and when he was asked of her, had replied, yes, yes, he could give hope now; she had youth in her favour, and a good constitution; and he trusted, nay, he felt tolerably sure, that she would recover.

It was astonishing how much anxiety and what general interest was excited about her. People who had hardly ever spoken to her or Mrs. Morland in their lives, came forward and offered their services, and thanked good Mrs. Morland for her benevolence, just as if they themselves had been benefited by it; they said she had come there a stranger among them, and had set them such a beautiful example, that they looked upon her as a public benefactor. It was quite cheering to see how much enthusiasm and good feeling was excited; and Mark Sopworth felt it comfortable to hide his own individual feelings in the general excitement; and without much difficulty, now everybody sent to inquire after her, he could present himself at Mrs. Morland's door without waiting for the privacy of the dusk; nor was he quite sure whether, if his family were in the town, they would not get as enthusiastic, not to say as heroic in love, as himself.

Lizzy was coming home, however, and Mark went in the afternoon of that day to inquire after Mary, that he might be able, as he said, to give his sister the latest intelligence when she came. Mrs. Morland was just coming out of her laboratory, where for the first time she had been busied since Mary's illness, and was then going with her sewing in her hand to her room, when Becky opened the front door to Mark Sopworth.

"Mary is better—really better!" said Mrs. Morland, quite gaily. She then told how calm she was, how grateful to everybody, and really looked so much like herself again, that it was quite a pleasure to see her. He looked so pleased by what she told him; and Mrs. Morland could not resist saying,

"Do come up and see her! Poor girl, it will make her so happy to see you! Go into the dining-room, Mr. Mark, while I go and prepare her for your visit!"

"Mary, dearest," said Mrs. Morland, going into her room, "here is a friend come to see you, but you shall not see him unless you promise to be quite calm; it is a friend who loves you dearly, and would be as sorry to agitate you as I should. Now, be a good girl, and keep calm. There, you look very pretty now! A night-cap really is very becoming; and I assure you," said she, kissing her, "that you never looked lovelier in your life. One can't help thinking of those things, you know; and I would not have let him come, if you had not looked so nice! There now, I think if you were a queen you could not be more in order!"

So said Mrs. Morland, happy in the thought that she was about to bring two loving hearts together; and then, with looks beaming with pleasure, went down and bade Mark follow her. He thought of Mary only, as he had seen her last when they had walked together in the fields below the town, as they often did; and, though he knew how ill she had been, he never had realised to his own mind the change which that illness had made upon her. What a shock, then, was it to him when he entered that darkened chamber, which seemed inexpressibly solemn, to find her lying more like a beautiful corpse than a living being, on the bed before him! The delicate hand which lay on the bed-clothes, but which the violence of fever had made weaker than a new-born child's slightly moved, and a faint blush passed over

the countenance, which welcomed him, however, with
a smile that seemed almost angelic.

He felt as if he could die for her; as if he could
defy both his family and Barbara Pocklington's;
and had it not been, perhaps, for the presence of Mrs.
Morland, he might have fallen on his knees by the
bed, and poured out the most passionate declarations
of love. He did not do so, however; he merely
seated himself in the chair by the bed, which Mrs.
Morland placed for him, and took her hand in his
without speaking one word; but to Mrs. Morland's
mind his silence and his manner spoke more than
words, and she was greatly pleased with him.

"I have been very ill," said Mary, at length, in a low
voice; "and it is so kind of you to come and see me."

He said a great deal; all which at the moment he
felt. He spoke of his sorrow, of his anxiety, of his
sympathy, and of his happiness now that she was
better. She would soon get better, he said; and
when spring came, and she could go out, she must
go, he said, to his mother; he would get her, he said,
to invite her for some weeks, and then she would be
well nursed, and soon would be strong again; Sommerton was so warm and pleasant, he said, and Mary
loved the country so much!

Thoughtless Mark Sopworth! And did he really
mean and believe all that he said? Perhaps not
entirely; but he was carried away by the impulse of
the moment: and while he thought to himself, "but
suppose my mother will not invite her"—the next
moment he thought, that perhaps he could persuade
her to do so—he really would try, and it was such a
pleasure to be generous and friendly!

Poor Mary, who saw in his behaviour everything to which her own heart could so joyfully respond, felt almost overwhelmed by happiness when he left her; and Mrs. Morland, perfectly satisfied that all was right, grew quite warm in praise of his lover-like conduct. " It is just what I expected from him," said she. " I knew he loved you; but now, for Heaven's sake, be quiet; don't excite yourself—you may again bring on fever!"

" When Mary is better," thought she to herself, I shall contrive that they shall be left together. The very first opportunity he will make a declaration, and then all will be as it should be."

Mary was indescribably happy; she believed that she was really loved. He of whom she had thought so much in her illness—nay, God forgive her, of whom she had thought when she believed that death was before her—was true to her, and worthy of her! She had done him some little injustice—she had doubted of his truth to her; but now! Those only who know the happiness of doing justice to one we love, can appreciate and understand what Mary's feelings were.

CHAPTER IX.

THE FALSE LOVE AND THE TRUE LOVE.

As Mark was leaving the door he met his own maid-servant. He had been seen entering Mrs. Morland's house, and was now sent for to his own. His sister was returned, and with her Barbara Pocklington, who

M

was come to spend the night with her. Barbara was
come to the town about a dress which was being made
for a subscription ball in a neighbouring town, which
would be given on the fifth of next month. The two
girls were almost in wild spirits. Lizzy wanted to go
to the ball too; she had made up her mind to do so;
but, before she went out about her dress, they
wanted to know if Mark would not go too. Mrs.
Sopworth would go with them as *chaperone* if her
son went, but not otherwise; if Mark did not go,
they must see if they two could go with the Websters;
but then the Websters were such horrid people! He
must go! He should go! and so it was no use his
thinking of anything else.

Mark, however, so immediately after his interview
with Mary, was not in any humour to think about
subscription balls, and more particularly of going to
one with Barbara Pocklington. He was vexed that
Barbara was come; was vexed with them both for
being so wild and foolish. " As if there was nothing
in this world," he said, " to think about but dancing
and jigging. He did not mean to go, and so they
need not ask him !"

" Well, if ever I heard the like !" exclaimed Barbara, not a little piqued.

' Oh, just as you please Mark," said his sister,
tossing her head : "there 'll be plenty of nice young
gentlemen there without you. Thank Heavens, neither
Barbara nor I would give a pin for dancing with you !"

The two girls went out to purchase their dresses,
making themselves sure that he would go after all;
and he sate down in an ill humour, vowing that he
never would go, and that was the long and short of it.

The next day his father came; and they two were closeted together. His father came, ostensibly, about the lease of the premises which was to be sold the next week by public auction, together with Mr. Crawley's effects, unless, in the meantime, it were disposed of by private contract. "It was," his father said, 'and so the son knew, "extremely desirable that it should be secured for him." The situation was the best in the town for trade; and no less than three different parties were in eager treaty about it, one of whom was a tea-dealer, the bitter rival in trade of Mark Sopworth himself. "There was no possiblity," Mr. Sopworth, sen. said, "of Morland's purchasing, but he had seen Mrs. Morland that day on the subject, and she was extremely anxious that Sopworth should be the purchaser; she had said a great many handsome things about his son : said she should prefer him to anybody, both for neighbour and land. lord; and that, for her part, and she would answer too for her husband, they would rather pay an advance of rent than leave, or have any changes. Mr. Sopworth, sen. was charmed with Mrs. Morland; she was a straight-forward, business-like person ; and, as everybody said she was making her husband's business answer, she would be a safe tenant."

Mark agreed to every word his father said: unquestionably the premises must be secured to him; he thought he had understood his father to say that they should be.

"Why, you see, Mark—" said the father, and then paused.

Mark fixed his eyes on his father, and wondered what he had to say.

The father then went on to say that, for his part, he could not conveniently raise the money ; his son had had already a good deal ; and it really was a serious thing advancing so much now-a-days. But he had, he said, spoken with Mr. Pocklington, or rather Mr. Pocklington had mentioned it to him.

Mark felt a sick sensation about his heart, and his father, who always spoke very slowly, went on. Mr. Pocklington had said that he had no objection to advance the money for the purchase of the lease, as he understood there was to be a family connection between them. "Now," said Mr. Sopworth, "this is a thing, Mark, that has my consent ; I have great respect for the Pocklingtons ; we've known one another all our lives. Your mother, too, wishes it above all things ; but I did not know that you and Barbara had come to such an understanding. She's a good girl, however ; and as I hate flirting and non- sense, you'd better get married pretty soon. Her father will give her the lease of the premises in part as her fortune ; and I think, as times go, you may reckon yourself a lucky fellow."

Mark began a stammering speech to his father, which his father could not understand ; at least it seemed to him that his son meant to say he had not made up his mind ; he should like a day or two to consider of it ; and that it was quite a mistake, if anybody said he and Barbara understood one another.

The old gentleman could hardly believe his ears ; he said that his wife and Lizzy, as well as old Ralph Pocklington, had told him so. What did his son mean ? Did he mean to say he was going to jilt Barbara ? If that was his meaning, why, then he

might take his own course! he, the father, would go
at once to the Pocklingtons and say he had nothing
to do with it, and he would cut off his son with a
shilling—that he would; and he would never stir
another step about the lease. Brockham might buy
it for anything he cared, and his son might·be a
bankrupt like old Crawley!

Mark was not at all prepared for this; it quite
frightened him, more especially as his father, taking
up his hat, thrust it violently on his head, and went
out, banging the door after him. It seemed to him
like a foretaste of the wrath to come, if he should
prefer Mary Wheeler to Barbara Pocklington.

"Well, I am in a pretty mess," thought he to
himself, "and, for the life of me, I do n't know what
I am to do!" He walked up and down the room in
great agitation, and at last looked out of his window
into the yard. The principal creditor of old Crawley,
and the rival tea-dealer, came out of Crawley's front
door. Mark felt as if the chance of the lease were
gone for ever, and that decided him as to what he
should do. He put on his hat and followed his
father to the Green Dragon, the inn at which he put
up when in town; but his father had mounted his
horse and was gone.

"Strike while the iron is hot!" thought the weak
young man to himself, doubting his own strength of
purpose; "if I see Mary Wheeler again, it may be
too late to run back. I never fairly proposed to her.
I must behave ill to one of them—either to Mary or
to Barbara. Mary I love the best, but Barbara has
money and friends who can help me; besides, it is
my father's will—so I decide!"

" It is my father's will ! " said he, many a time
to himself, " so it is no fault of mine ! "

.. His father was pacified by his wise decision, as he
called it, and his mother said she had always known,
ever since Barbara was a child, that it would be a
match between Mark and her ; and nothing could
equal the good humour and apparent satisfaction both
of father and mother. The next morning he went
to the Pocklingtons and made his declaration in due
form ; the next evening the two families drank tea
together ; the morning afterwards the lease was
purchased by private contract by old Sopworth, for
his son, with old Pocklington's money ; and, on the
5th of February, the three young people and the two
mothers went, as gay as could be, in a coach hired
for the occasion, to the subscription ball.

Mary Wheeler was recovering daily : nay, indeed,
ever since that afternoon of Mark Sopworth's visit,
she had recovered strength as if by magic. The first
days of February were mild and genial, and the good
Dr. Wentworth said that on the morrow she might
leave her bed for an hour or two, and, supported by
pillows, take her tea while seated in the great easy
chair.

The sun shone into the chamber warm and cheerfully, and Mrs. Morland, who had received a most
happy, satisfactory letter from her husband, went
again into her laboratory to prepare a fresh supply
for the demand which was now being made on all
hands for their articles.

Mary sat, in her long white wrapping-gown, in
the easy-chair, occupying herself partly by reading
and partly by thoughts which were not anxious. She

had left off her night-cap, and had that day, for the
first time since her illness, arranged her lovely hair
in its usual mode. She looked more than ordinarily
interesting, for she was full of grateful and affectionate
feeling, and looked both good and happy.

The door opened, and Becky announced Dr. Wentworth. It always had been a pleasure to see him,
but at this moment it was, Mary knew not why,
even more so than usual. Agreeable, however, as
had been his coming, he did not stay very long ; and
Mrs. Morland, who was coming up stairs with a
letter in her hand, met him as he went out. The
letter which she held in her hand was one of great
importance to Mary, but yet it was not of that of
which Mrs. Morland spoke first.

" What in the world is amiss with Dr. Wentworth ?" asked she ; " and you, Mary ?—in tears, I
declare."

Mary wept still. " The excellent, noble, generous
man !" exclaimed she, at length, " to think only of
his loving me—of his asking me to become his wife !"

Mrs. Morland looked at her earnestly without
speaking.

" What am I to do, Mrs. Morland ?" asked she ;
" I that would not give pain to any human being if
I could help it—what pain and distress have I not
given to him !"

" And have you really refused him !" exclaimed
Mrs. Morland. " Really and truly refused Dr. Wentworth !"

" I have indeed !" said Mary, " how could I do
otherwise ?"

Mrs. Morland again fixed her eyes on Mary and
looked troubled.

" But for one person," said Mary, " I could have loved him—and then how happy, how inexpressibly happy and fortunate I should have been!—but you know I could not."

Mrs. Morland felt angry : perhaps it was unrea-sonable, but still she certainly felt angry.

" Well Mary," said she, " you have done a most foolish thing, and what, if you really have done it, which I can hardly bring my mind to conceive, you will repent to the last day of your life !"

"Oh Mrs. Morland!" said Mary, "how can you say so—and how can you make me thus miserable? My heart aches for Dr. Wentworth ; I honour and esteem him, and admire his generosity beyond words!"

" Admire and esteem !" repeated Mrs. Morland, in a tone of such bitter mockery as cut her to the heart—" why, Mary Wheeler, there is not a girl in the town, hardly in the country, who would not be ennobled by marrying Dr. Wentworth.   He is a gentleman, and not only that, but is so good and so rich—and then you have refused him just for a paltry tea-dealer !"

She threw the letter down upon the table, and walked hastily up and down the room, never sympa-thising with the poor girl, who felt, even more than she did, the pain of having given pain to a noble heart.

" Dearest Mrs. Morland," said Mary at length, "what in the world was I to do? You know all about Mark as well as I do ; you think highly of him—you said you did.   I confess, before Heaven and you, to loving him sincerely ; how then could I have accepted Dr. Wentworth ? And as to Mark being only a tea-dealer, why, what am I? Poor as a beggar! and it is generous in him to love me and to be willing, as I believe he is, to make me his wife. Oh Mrs. Morland, think only dispassionately about it, and would you not really have despised me, as I am sure I should have despised myself, if I had accepted Dr. Wentworth merely because he was a richer man and of higher station? And, good and noble and right-minded as Dr. Wentworth is, I am sure he would not have wished me to do otherwise, nor could he have respected me if I had!"

"You are right! you are right, dear Mary," said Mrs. Morland, throwing her arms round her neck; "I only hope and trust that Mr. Sopworth may deserve love as noble and disinterested as yours!"

Mary sighed deeply, for amid her deep, deep sympathy with her rejected lover, all at once the sense came over her soul that as yet the preferred lover had not proposed.

"I wish, however," said Mrs. Morland, that this had not happened, for Dr. Wentworth is one in ten thousand; and though my own heart tells me that you have done right, I am anything but satisfied. This affair, however, has put something out of my head—something very pleasant, and which you will like to hear."

"You have a letter, then, from Mr. Morland?' said Mary, as she took it up again.

"No," returned she; "but do you know this handwriting?" asked she, showing her the direction Mary did not. "Ah, that is odd," said she; "but you must know that, when you were so ill, I wrote to the clergyman of Morton, to inquire if that good

grand-uncle, and aunt Fielding, of whom you told
me so much, were still living, and in case they were,
I begged him to give them my letter. In my letter
I told them all about you ; of your uncle's failure,
and of your illness, and a great deal more than I choose
to tell you just now, because it was all praise ;—
and I, just now, am not so very well pleased with
you," said she, smiling. Mary listened breathlessly,
and she continued. " I thought it very odd that I
did not receive an answer ; but, however, this is
inclosed in one from the clergyman, who tells me
that this village is properly Morton-le-Wold, and
that my letter had been travelling to all the Mor-
tons in three or four counties, before it reached its
destination ; however, it got right at last, and here,
then, is a letter from your dear old uncle himself,
which I will read to you :—

" *Morton-le-Wold, January* 28, 183—.
" Dear Madam,
" Thank you for yours. I and my wife are still
living, thank God, and in tolerable health. What
you write of the dear child has grieved us greatly.
We always understood Mr. Joseph Crawley to be,
not only a man of substance, but of great respectability. May the Almighty bless you for finding a
home for the fatherless and motherless ! We shall
be greatly pleased to have the dear child with us ;
we remember her well, and all her little affectionate
ways. She, and poor Edward, were the offspring of
upright and God-fearing people ; and while we have
bread to eat, they shall never want.

" We shall hope to hear from you again by return

of post, as, from what you write of her illness, we
are full of anxiety about her. I will, if you think
it advisable, or if it would be any comfort to her,
come over to see her, for I am hearty, though somewhat in years, and rather rheumatic; but should
not fear a journey, the season being so mild, and
especially if it would be any comfort to her who is
so dear to us both..

"It is, indeed, a great pleasure, that she remembers
us with so much affection. Tell her not to be cast
down, for that she shall have a home with us, and
should have had that long ago, had we not thought
her better provided for than with us. She will be
a great comfort to us in our old age; and my wife,
who begs me to send her love to her, is quite impatient that I should set off for her. But before I do
that, it is best that we hear again from you.

"With respectful compliments from my wife, and
our most sincere thanks for the kindness you have
shown to one who is so dear to us, which truly
verifies the words of the Psalmist, ' I have been
young, and now I am old, yet I never saw the
righteous forsaken, or his seed begging bread,'

   " Believe me, dear Madam,

  " Yours very faithfully, and gratefully,

    " BERNARD FIELDING."

"To Mrs. George Morland,
 "in W——."

It is impossible to say what happiness this letter
infused into Mary's heart. The remembrance of
those dear old relatives had lived in her mind as a
beautiful part of that beautiful dream of childhood,

which, in the hard realities of her after experience
seemed to have passed away for ever; but here
again were they all unexpectedly presented before
her. It seemed as if the clouds of life were passing
away, and the true and the kind were opening their
arms to receive her.

" What a kind, thoughtful, and active friend have
you not been for me," said Mary, addressing Mrs.
Morland, "and for how much, indeed, have I not
to thank God!" She could say no more, but clasp-
ing her hands before her face, she poured forth silent
thanksgiving to her Father in heaven.

She was too much excited by all the events of the
day, to be able to write to the old people. Mrs.
Morland, therefore, undertook to make the immediate reply.

She could not do other than write cheerfully, for
she had much good news to communicate. Mary
was better; was now out of all danger, and was made
perfectly happy by this prospect of reunion with
them. She begged to think of them as beloved
parents, to whom she might show a daughter's duty
and affection, and she looked forward impatiently to
the day when she might be received under their
roof. So much was written as dictated by Mary
herself; and then, Mrs. Morland added, that until
the weather was quite warm and settled, and until
Mary's health was quite established, she must
remain where she was. Mrs. Morland said, that
she was extremely attached to her, and would not
readily have consented to part with her, did she not
feel that relations so excellent as these, and to
whom Mary herself was so warmly attached, had a

prior claim to her. She would be, she said, a blessing and a happiness to them ; and then, she wrote about all her virtues, and her good qualities, which, seeing we know them all so well, need not be repeated.

Poor Mary had been so much excited that day, as not to be able to sit upon the morrow She suffered from intolerable headache ; and, spite of the happiness which her uncle Fielding's letter had occasioned, there was a something unsatisfactory in her own feelings. It was now a fortnight since that afternoon when Mark Sopworth had sat with her; and since that day, only occasional inquiries after her health, had shown that he kept her in remembrance.

Mrs. Morland had seen him many times since then, but that only on business; it is true that he had always spoken of Mary with an appearance of the same interest as formerly, and that had satisfied her. She was, however, very closely occupied at this time by her own business, which, as we have before said, began to promise the most complete success. Sometimes for whole days she was occupied in her laboratory, and then again in seeing that orders were made up and sent off. Old Matthew was fully employed in the heavier work, as in Mr. Nixon's days, and a young man, whom her uncle had strongly recommended, and sent to her, served her as warehouseman. She had, indeed, enough to do to attend to her own affairs ; and, had she been a selfish person, she would have said so ; but as it was, she found time not only to think about Mary, but to be a little uneasy also on her account.

It was odd, she thought, that, if Mark Sopworth

N

really was sincere in all he said, and really meant all
his behaviour implied, that he never came to the house
excepting on business; and that he always declined
her invitations to stay, though by staying he might
have the opportunity of seeing and talking with the
girl he professed to love. There was something unsatisfactory in it, which she attributed to the influence
of his sister, who had now, for a long time, behaved
towards Mary with great coldness. She gave him
the benefit of everything in his favour; he had been
so occupied about the lease, but now that that was
completed, she felt assured that he would soon set
all things right.

Two or three days more went on, but no Mark
Sopworth made his appearance, nor was he now to
be seen when she looked out of her front door,
standing, as usual, at the desk in his backshop
writing, or with the pen behind his ear.

"I'll certainly contrive to speak with him,"
thought she, one day. "I'll call for a pound of tea,
or I'll make up some errand about the lease; but I
really must have some opportunity of talking with
him!"

Whilst she was thinking thus, Becky, who was
laying the cloth for dinner, began to tell what was
the *on dit* of the Barkers' Sarah, and the Sopworths'
Ann. Mr. Mark Sopworth was going to be married
at Midsummer; he had bought the whole premises,
and workmen were even now beginning to get the
place in order. He was going to live in old Crawley's house.

"Indeed!" said Mrs. Morland; "and to whom is
he going to be married, Becky?"

"To Miss Barbara Pocklington," returned she.

"Indeed!" again said Mrs. Morland.

"So they say," continued Becky, "and I believe so myself. They say it is all a settled thing; and only last night he came home from somewhere, where he had been with her to a ball. It's a sin and a shame," said Becky, looking quite angry, "after all the notice he took of Miss Wheeler, to serve her so; and if I were you and her, I'd never let him darken my doors again as long as I lived! But she's a deal too good for him—that she is," said poor Becky, in a self-consoling tone—"a world too good for him; and so I said to Ann, 'He's no such great shakes,' says I, 'after all, and there's plenty, better than him, as will jump at her!'"

"I think so too, Becky," said Mrs. Morland; "but I advise you, nevertheless, not to talk about it with the servants—it is a great deal better not!"

"No, I've had my say," said Becky, "and I shall say no more; only this I *will* stick to, that, if ever a young lady had a right to think a man loved her, why, it was Miss Wheeler. He could not let her go out of the house, but he must follow her; and then, as long as old Crawley was thought to be rich, all his folks was making so much of her. It's been so ever since they came to the shop; nothing was too good for her then. I hate to see such money-worship!— But let him take his Miss Barbara! he'll have enough of his bargain before he's been a married man twelve months! But, bless me, my mutton will be burnt to a coal!" said Becky, cutting short her tirade, and hurrying out into the kitchen.

Mrs. Morland heard first from one, and then from

another, the same thing as Becky had told her: Mark Sopworth was to be married at Midsummer, and was getting ready his house to receive his wife. She had not seen him for a·long time, that is for several days, and she suspected, therefore, that he avoided seeing her. She went out, however, one afternoon, and met him point-blank in turning a corner, not far from his house.

"Good afternoon! Mr. Mark," said she, stopping him; "we have seen nothing of you of late. You are so busy preparing your new house, I hear," said she, as he made no answer, and she was determined he should not escape.

He turned alternately pale, and then red: stammered something, and looked uneasy.

"The good people of W—," continued she gaily, "are infinitely obliged to you for giving them something to talk of."

"To talk of!" repeated he; "what do they talk of?"

"Nay, you must not come to me for the news," said Mrs. Morland, smiling; "you know what everybody is saying!"

"No, upon my word! No, I protest! What do you mean?" stammered he, looking an object of almost pitiable confusion. "But — but — how is Miss Wheeler?" asked he, endeavouring, but in vain, to speak in an assured tone of voice.

"Very much better—nay, indeed quite well!" returned Mrs. Morland, not quite adhering to the strict truth, but determined to convince him, if possible, that his faithlessness affected her but very little.

He made no reply, but abruptly left her, blessing his stars that he had got away.

"He knows himself to be a villain!" said Mrs. Morland, as she walked onward; "a mean, pitiful sneak as he is—I despise him from my very soul!"

As she entered her own door again, she saw him sitting as usual at his desk in his back shop, with his chin resting on both his hands. "The worst I wish for him," thought she, "is, that he may just have sense enough left to feel what a despicable being he is!"

Whatever his feelings might be, the very next time Mrs. Morland went out of her door, she saw that a green silk curtain was put half way up the back shop window, and thus the desk and its occupant was concealed from view. "It's an excellent thing!" said she to herself, "for I hate to see him; and I would not for the world that poor Mary, just for the short time she has to stay here, should be annoyed by seeing him!"

"Thank Heaven," said Sopworth to himself that afternoon, as he sat resting his chin on his hands— "Thank Heaven that Mary Wheeler has nobody to take up her quarrel! Both her cue and Mrs. Morland's, will be to say as little about it as possible. Nobody ever can say that I made her a direct offer! Like her, I certainly did; and I would be glad enough to change Barbara for her; but that can't be. Barbara's a handsome girl; and, as to Mary, it's only just now that I think so much about it. When I have seen her a time or two it will all be nothing: but as for that, at present I'd rather go ten miles round than meet even Mrs. Morland!"

The fear of seeing either Mrs. Morland or Mary, made him have the green blind put up; and the

unpleasant feeling of having met Mrs. Morland so
unhinged him, that he set off the day following to
Sommerton, and on his way there resolved to
embrace the offer which young Pocklington had
made him, to go out for a couple of days snipe-
shooting. " I 'll come back on Wednesday morning,"
said he, "for market, and by that time I shall have
got up my spirits again."

Not a word was said by Mrs. Morland to Mary of
what Becky had told her, and of what all the world
said ; nor yet did she tell her of her meeting with
Mark Sopworth. Poor Mary suffered dreadfully
from head-ache, and, poorly as she continued, Dr.
Wentworth never came to see her. It is impossible
to say how much this circumstance troubled her.
She feared that she had lost his esteem and friendship
for ever, and she thought of him continually.

" I should be so glad to hear his carriage stop as it
used to do ! " thought she many a time ; " but it is
not likely he will ever come to see me again. I
know I have offended him ; and yet, if he could only
understand my feelings—could know how I admire
and esteem him—he would not blame me !"

Fear lest she had lost his friendship for ever,
almost equally shared her mind with the one thought
which otherwise would have occupied it altogether,—
and that was, that Mark Sopworth never came near
her, never sent even to inquire after her, that she
heard of.

No wonder was it that her head became so
intolerably bad. One Sunday afternoon she lay
with vinegar cloths on her forehead, to allay the
throbbing pain there. It was at the end of February,

wet and cheerless, and the twilight seemed to come
on as early as on the shortest day. Mrs. Morland
sat reading in a volume of sermons by the fire, and
Mary lay on her bed, the silent tears, which she did
not wipe away, trickling down to the pillow. Mrs.
Morland was called out of the room, and in about a
quarter of an hour returned.

"Dr. Wentworth has been to inquire after you,
dear," said she.

"Thank God!" returned Mary, taking up her
handkerchief and wiping away the tears, which now
flowed with hysterical violence; "I feared he would
never come near me again!"

"He has sent every day to inquire after you,"
returned Mrs. Morland, without noticing Mary's
emotion; "I have not seen him, however, since that
day till now, and really, poor fellow, he looks so ill!"

Mary covered her face with her handkerchief, and
sobbed bitterly.

"For Heaven's sake be calm, Mary!" said Mrs.
Morland; "what is to become of your poor head if
you cry thus? He desires you may be kept calm,
and your forehead cool," said she, dipping a fresh
cloth in the vinegar. "Bless me, how burning hot
your forehead is," added she, taking the other away.

"And it throbs dreadfully," said Mary. "Thank
you; how deliciously cool it now is!" added she,
when the fresh linen was laid on. "But oh, Mrs.
Morland," said she, seizing her hand, "I do so wish
my mind could be made easy! I do wish I could
honestly and truly know what you think—"

She paused, and Mrs. Morland, who understood
her meaning perfectly, replied, "Not to-day, dear
Mary, will I talk of anything that can agitate you;

keep quiet—do not dwell on any painful or disquiet-
ing thought, and if there be one thing in this world
that is calmly and soothingly pleasant to think of,
think of it, or I will talk to you of it, calmly and
softly, just as I think best; but not one word to-day
either about Dr. Wentworth or Mr. Sopworth."

" I have been thinking a great deal," said Mary,
" of my good uncle and aunt Fielding. I shall be
so glad to see them; and I think—I have thought so
for several days—that if you would not think it
ungrateful, I should like to leave W— altogether,
and go to Morton."

Mrs. Morland knew what the true spring of these
thoughts was, and, stooping down and kissing her,
she replied, "Yes, love, and so I think. In Spring
the country is so pleasant, and Morton, you say, is
so pretty; and then, those good old people are so
kind, and love you so much! You shall go, and
then, when you are better, and quite strong, perhaps
next Christmas, you shall come here again on a visit
to me."

Mary pressed her hand, but made no reply.

" You shall write me long letters from Morton,"
continued Mrs. Morland—"long letters, which to me,
living in the close-built town, stoving all day down
in my laboratory, will come breathing of the country
like fresh fruits or flowers. You shall study music
with the good old uncle, and learn all kind of household accomplishments from the dear old aunt! Yes,
dear girl—jesting apart—it will be a holy and a heal-
ing life for you. We will get all your clothes in order,
and when the warmer weather comes we will send
for the good old uncle to fetch you."

CHAPTER X.

PARTING AND MEETING.

Not a word ever passed between Mrs. Morland and Mary, respecting Mark Sopworth and his false love. When she left her chamber for the first time, and went into the dining-room, she saw, through the staircase window, the workmen busily employed on the premises which her uncle had occupied, and Mark Sopworth, without his hat, standing there. He was pointing out something about the upper story to young Pocklington, who was with him; but not a word did Mary say, although a deep sigh escaped her, and Mrs. Morland could not help remarking the deathly paleness which overspread her countenance, and robbed every tinge of colour from her lips.

She had come to know, but Mrs. Morland never discovered how, that he was about to be married to Barbara Pocklington; she mentioned it once, but never again, and Mrs. Morland used all the means in her power to divert her thoughts and enliven her.

March came and passed, and then came April with flowers and budding leaves; but Mary was still an invalid. Her sickness, however, was more of the mind than the body, and both she and her friend unanimously agreed that the time was now come when she must go to Morton. She had not yet been out of the house; she had a morbid dread of it; and Mrs. Morland, though she wished it, and

thought it would be much better if she had—nay,
even that she had accustomed herself to see Sopworth, had not the heart to urge it.

All the preparations necessary for her departure
were made ; the great leathern trunk lent to her by
her friend, stood in her chamber ready filled, and
the carpet-bag, lent also, out of Mr. Morland's inexhaustible store of such things, lay upon it.   Old Mr.
Fielding was to come the next day; he was to
remain with them one day, and on the following.
Mary was to commence her journey.

If the name of Sopworth was carefully avoided by
them, no less so was that of Dr. Wentworth.   Mary
had never seen him since the day when he had
declared to her his passion.   A great change since
then had taken place in her life's prospects.   Mrs.
Morland wished, above all things, that she could
again bring about the affair between them : but in
the then sensitive state of Mary's feelings, she would
not even speak of him, and, as regarded himself, if
he even were desirous of renewing his suit, which his
now total absence hardly, perhaps, seemed to promise, he was not exactly the person that anybody
could   suggest   anything to, especially a delicate
affair like this.   Mrs. Morland, therefore, thought
that everything must be left to take its own course;
but, said she to herself many a time, " If there be
one thing more than another that makes me detest
Sopworth, it is, that he has made Mary lose a husband like Dr. Wentworth."

Both Mrs. Morland and Mary that evening were
very low-spirited ; and, had it not been that a foreign
letter came in quite unexpectedly, directed to Mrs.

Morland for Mary, they certainly would both have wept to keep each other company. The letter was from Ned, and was written from the Cape of Good Hope, and was such a letter as none but a heart like his could dictate — affectionate, full of sound good sense, and taking, at the same time, the most cheerful views of life. He said that this would be his last voyage as ship's apprentice; and, unlike his former voyages, this would enable him to return to England by the end of the year. In the meantime he said—for he had been thinking much and seriously on his sister's prospects—he wished her to write to their relations the Fieldings, and if they still lived, to solicit a home with them, where he would visit her on his return. But if they lived not, he besought her to ask the same from Mrs. Morland: and, as to money, he said he should soon be in the receipt of sufficient to pay whatever had been incurred for her; and, please God he again reached England, they would have many a merry hour together, and laugh at all old troubles.

Had the letter been the voice of an angel from heaven, it could not have produced a more happy effect than it did. For the first time for these many months, Mary felt perfectly cheerful. In comparison with Sopworth, how true-hearted and straightforward did Ned seem, while, in point of character and goodness, he lost nothing when compared with the excellent Dr. Wentworth.

The evening really was cheerful; Mrs. Morland laughed and told amusing anecdotes; Mary smiled, and felt as if, some time or other, she might be perhaps again light-hearted.

In the course of the next afternoon, she heard Mrs. Morland bring some one into the passage—somebody was taking off a great-coat—it might be her uncle; she rushed to the door the very moment that it was opened, and the bending figure of an old, but not feeble man, with strongly marked, but most singularly mild and intelligent countenance, and snowy white hair which fell upon his shoulders, met her eye. It was her uncle, and the next moment she was clasped in his arms. He did not speak for some time, but gazed tenderly into her face. " She is so like her mother!" said he at length, wiping a tear away, and turning to Mrs. Morland; " so very like her poor dear mother!" He then put her back at arm's length, and surveyed her from head to foot. "She was but a little child," said he, " when she parted from us: she is now grown tall, poor thing! and very like her mother!" He kissed her again and again, and seemed greatly pleased with her.

It was indeed a happy meeting, and the kindly cheerful spirit of the dear old man operated most beneficially on her mind, even in the course of a few hours.

Mr. Fielding had most correct notions with regard to money matters. He had come prepared to discharge all debts which had been incurred on account of his niece—more especially as regarded medical attendance. As yet, Dr. Wentworth had had no fee. He had not received it in the first instance, and after circumstances had made Mrs. Morland feel some delicacy, at least while Mary remained with her, in renewing the subject with him. But Mr.

Fielding, of course, knew nothing of all this; and, after Mrs. Morland had refused to receive one single penny for the expense she herself had incurred, he set out to discharge the just debt to the good physician, and at the same time to express his thanks to him, for both Mary and Mrs. Morland had spoken of his extreme kindness.

Poor Mary! how her heart beat as he set out, soon after nine, that he might be sure of finding him at home, before he went round to his patients; and how impatient was she, too, for his return, and yet at the same time afraid of his returning too soon, for then she should fear he had not seen him; and someway she did not know how she felt. She would have liked, of all things, to have seen him once again before she left, to have known at least that they two parted friends.

Her uncle at last came back: there was an expression of pleasure in his countenance, as he entered the room, which indicated that his interview had given him satisfaction. He was, like everybody else, charmed with Dr. Wentworth, for he was one who, though he was old, could understand and appreciate fully a noble and uncommon character, and such he felt Dr. Wentworth to be. Every word which he spoke gave both pleasure and pain to poor Mary.

Dr Wentworth, he said, had refused a fee, and that so peremptorily, that he could not think of urging it. He had inquired most particularly after his niece; had warmly approved of her removal into the country; he said that she required change of scene and perfect repose of mind. He had asked, too, of their intended mode of travelling; and, as there was no direct coach from W—, and they must take a hired conveyance the two first stages, and it was altogether a long fatiguing day's journey, he had proposed to send his own close carriage with them till they took the coach, which he said would be better for an invalid than any hired carriage. Mr. Fielding was delighted with the benevolence of the offer, and could talk of nothing else all the morning but the extreme kindness and consideration of that good physician. He thought his niece particularly fortunate in such a medical attendant; he did not wonder at her getting better, particularly when she had a nurse like Mrs. Morland.

Mr. Fielding and Mrs. Morland talked of old Crawley, and of the house in which he lived; and when the old gentleman set out in the afternoon to look about him, he walked down the court to take a survey of the house in which his poor niece had experienced so much unhappiness. Mr. Mark Sopworth was with his workpeople, and the old gentleman began to talk with him. He told who he was, and that he was come to fetch his great-niece away; she was a very good girl, he said, and he thanked God that he had it in his power to provide for her. Sopworth moved first here, and then there; felt anything but at his ease, and wished the old gentleman would go. He would almost have told him to remove himself, for nothing made him so uncomfortable as to hear Mary Wheeler talked of; and as this was her uncle, he did not know how much of his

miserable weakness—not to call it by a worse name
—had been revealed to him. Poor old gentleman,
nothing, however, did he know to Mark Sopworth's
disadvantage, nor indeed did he know who Mark
Sopworth was; but thinking that this person, let
him be whoever he would, was either out of humour,
or naturally uncivil, he turned himself about, and
walked slowly up the court again.

" Why, is not that old fellow from Morton-le-wold,
in Devonshire ?" asked a commercial traveller who
dealt in spices, and who, not finding Sopworth in his
shop, had followed him here. " It is, as sure as I'm
alive! Why, he is as rich as a Jew ; I heard so at
Exeter this week. He lives at Morton like a miser,
and does not spend fifty pounds a year: but he's
laying up money by thousands !"

Not one word of all this was true, excepting that
he lived at Morton, and that the commercial traveller
had seen him in Exeter, where he had been the week
before ; but the traveller was a wit, and his wit
many a time showed itself by rhodomontading stories
which he made up on the occasion. " I hope you
have not offended the old fellow," said he, " for they
say he is looking out for an heir ; I laid myself out
to please him last week, but, unfortunately, I dropped
the ashes of my cigar into his negus, and the ashes of
a cigar are his aversion, so I lost my chance !"

Had there been the most bitter malice in the mind
of the commercial traveller against Mr. Mark Sopworth, he could not have tortured him worse than
he did by all this. " Perhaps, then," thought he to
himself, " Mary Wheeler after all may be a great

heiress—may be richer a hundred times than Barbara Pocklington!"

In the early morning, before the shops were yet open—except to the youngest apprentices, who were cleaning outsides of windows and such things—a private close carriage conveyed away from the entry-end Mary Wheeler and her uncle. Ann, the Sopworths' servant, told this at breakfast. "It was a very handsome carriage," she said, "every bit as handsome as Dr. Wentworth's."

"It was Dr. Wentworth's," said the youngest apprentice.

"Yes, that it was, and Dr. Wentworth's horses too," said the youngest apprentice but one.

Sopworth said nothing at all, but felt as if the dry toast he was eating, spite of all the butter which he had laid thickly upon it, would stick in his throat, for he made no doubt whatever but that it was in the private carriage of the rich old uncle, and not that of Dr. Wentworth, which she had been conveyed away.

CHAPTER XI.

THE OLD FRIENDS AND THE OLD HOME.

MARY wrote to her dear friend Mrs. Morland; and we think we cannot oblige our readers more than by giving a long extract from a letter, dated in the early part of May.

"By my last," she wrote, "you would know how well this place and this quiet country life agree with me. The weather has completely changed within the last fortnight, and all is like Paradise around me. It is the Morton of my childhood; and, thank Heaven, the peace of mind, if not the joyous-heartedness of childhood, seems to have returned.

"But you ask me of my dear uncle and aunt How could I write so hastily, or be so completely self-absorbed as to say so little of them in my last? I have found them as simple, and kind, and good, as my memory had chronicled them. In one or two little particulars, however, their style of living is changed,—for instance, they keep a woman-servant now; and the grand piano, which is a far finer and nobler instrument than ever my childhood imagined it, stands now in the parlour, which has become their daily sitting-room, instead of the kitchen, as formerly. The furniture, however, is the most simple that can be imagined; and it really seems most singularly strange, not to say startling, to see a magnificent instrument like this standing in so humble an apartment. 'The only thing,' says my uncle many a time, 'for which I covet a large house, or at least one large and noble room, is to hold my piano, and to do justice to its power.' Poor dear old man, he sometimes talks of sinking some part of his income in order to erect such a room, and if he had only himself to think of and care for, he would do it. He would, I am sure, sleep on a chaff-bed, and live on bread and water, to purchase the full enjoyment of music; but then, he is so deeply attached to his wife, thinks so much for her, and studies her comforts so earnestly, that I am sure he will never do it.

He has told me often, and that with tears in his eyes, that it was she who proposed and induced him to purchase this magnificent instrument, though it obliged them for ten years to deprive themselves of their few luxuries, and to practise the greatest economy and self-denial. It was during this time that I knew them as a child, and when they lived without a servant. She never complained, he has told me, all that time, though, when he saw her hands becoming coarse with hard household work, he felt many a bitter reproach on himself. She loves music, however, as well as her husband, and is so proud of his great skill, that I am sure she had always her exceeding great reward ; but I cannot tell you how the contemplation of their virtues, and their beautiful unselfish attachment to each other, has strengthened and gladdened my heart. If my aunt is not in the room, my uncle seems not wholly satisfied, though seated at his instrument ; if the door opens, he instantly looks round, for he feels that he yet fails of something, and that is the presence of his wife : but when she comes in, and is seated by him, he gives himself up with undivided soul to the full enthusiasm of his art, and plays superbly.

" He is not at all satisfied with my playing. I learned, he says—and that is true—from inferior masters, and my playing is full of faults. I have begun to study industriously under him, and to sing also ; and, with such a master to teach, and such an instrument to practise upon, I hope to make something out.

" I must relate to you an anecdote of my uncle, to prove to you how good a man he is. I told you, I think, of the misunderstanding which, as a child, I recollected to exist between my uncle and the organist of the parish church. He was the only person who lived in strife with the dear old man ; he was of a most violent temper, and, feeling my uncle's superiority to himself in music, regarded him always ae.a rival, and that more especially after there had been an attempt on the part of the clergyman, and some of the more respectable parishioners, to displace him in favour of my uncle. But my uncle declined to accept the offer, for the organist was a poor man with a family, and the office was of consequence to him. The organist, however, never gave him credit for his forbearance, but lived on in bitter enmity with him ; which was a cause of great regret to my uncle, more particularly as, though the organist was but an indifferent musician himself, his youngest son exhibited no ordinary talent, and was intended by his father to succeed him in his office. My uncle was greatly interested in the youth ; he was, poor fellow, of a sickly constitution, and afflicted with so great a weakness in his back as to produce gradually a painful deformity. My uncle wished to have given the poor youth instruction, but the obstinate unfriendliness of the father prevented this. At length the organist fell sick, and lay on his death-bed, and then my uncle went to him, and besought that all animosity might cease from his mind, promising that he would promote in every possible way the advancement and worldly advantage of his afflicted son. The heart of the dying man was touched: this was an instance of forgiveness and Christian love which far surpassed his belief: yet, while it affected him most deeply, it blessed and consoled his death-bed. My uncle saw him every day till he died, and his last words were, ' May God Almighty be only as merciful to me as Mr. Fielding!'

" My uncle fulfilled his promise, the poor youth came for a year or two to him daily, and evinced extraordinary talent for his art, while my uncle became almost as much attached to him as if he were his son. At length, however, his spine was affected, and he could not leave the house; my uncle then went to him, and still continues to do so daily, for the poor fellow now is in the last stage of consumption, and cannot himself touch the instrument, but my uncle sits for hours in his room, and plays to him, which is his greatest delight; he will die, no doubt, listening to his music. The doctor says he cannot continue long, and not a day, let the weather be what it may, passes without my uncle visiting him.

" Have I not, my dear friend, reason to be proud of my dear old relatives?

" You ask me of the house in which I was born—the old school-house. Alas! it is an altered place now, and perhaps it is as well it should be so, for had the ivy still covered the end up to the very chimneys, and had the monthly roses and the trumpet honeysuckle still been trained up the front, and the sheds of auriculas and hyacinths still stood down the length of the garden, it would have reminded me almost too painfully of my parents; but it has no look of home about it now. The schoolmaster, who is a fat man, and an old bachelor, fancied the ivy made the house damp, and found roses and honey-suckles too much trouble to keep well trained, so he had them all cleared away; the house was new-roofed and stuccoed, and made as trim as a new building, with the school-house to match. Beside all this, he discovered that all those great elms and limes which grew round about and in the front, made the school dark, so he persuaded the parish to cut down four of them, and thus had plenty of light both winter and summer. Instead of prize-flowers, he grows pink-eyed potatoes, the richest marrow-fats in the parish, and pumpkins, which are the wonder of half the county, for he loves good eating above all things; but he brings the boys on, say all the villagers, and the squire is satisfied with him, and so is the clergyman, and thus whatever he does is right. It grieved me, however, to see all these changes, and I protested that he was a Goth; but he sent me the other day a bushel of new potatoes, and a kind mes-sage to come whenever I liked, and see ' his improve-ments;' so I think the man has a good heart, after all, and, like everybody else—I mean to be satisfied with him.

"My uncle's income, as I told you, is about eighty pounds a year. I must do something for my own maintenance; for, though they begrudge me nothing, I cannot bear to encumber them in any way, or oblige them to deprive themselves of any comforts on my account. Besides all this, as a matter of necessary duty to myself, I must keep my mind occupied, and that as much as possible, with things disconnected with myself. I must have full employment, and that of such a character as, while it demands exertion on my part, leaves me no time to dwell on painful and engrossing, and at the same time enfeebling subjects. I am not, my dearest friend, as yet strong either in mind or body, but, thank God, light seems breaking in around me; I begin to see what is best for me, and what it is my duty to do. I am reconciled to much that at one time seemed bitter to me as death. I am, too, at peace with myself; and to have peace with one's self, to see clearly what is one's duty, and to feel a willingness to do it, is having advanced many steps on the right path. Yes, my best friend, the worst is over now; all will in time be right, and in time, I doubt not, I shall see that all has been indeed for the best. But, in the meantime, I must find active and constant employment, and this, not only as a duty to myself, but to my excellent relations also.

"My present idea is to propose myself as daily governess to Mrs. Morton, the lady of the squire, for her two little girls. I love children, and these are amiable and tractable; we are already good friends, for the squire's family, as well as the clergyman's, have shown me great kindness; and I feel that I could make these children love me, and, perhaps, be useful to them. Their mother is inquiring for a governess; I will go this very day and propose myself. When I take up my pen again, I will tell you the result.

"*The morrow.*—I went yesterday to the hall.

It is all delightfully settled; but you shall hear. I knew that a governess was wanted, and therefore I had no difficulty in proposing myself, especially as the children are quite young, the eldest being but ten. To my great joy, I found my proposal gladly accepted. Mrs. Morton expressed the greatest pleasure; said many flattering things to me, and proposed• to give me five-and-thirty pounds a year, which is more than I expected. I am to enter on my office immediately. She has heard me play, and, being a less severe critic than my uncle, commends my playing greatly. I commence my duties at 9 o'clock on Monday morning. I am to walk with the children from twelve to one; dine with them at one; walk again with them for an hour in the afternoon, if the weather is fine; and whatever I am required to teach as yet, I understand tolerably well. At six o'clock I return home for the evening. I shall thus have several hours each day to spend with my uncle and aunt, and to practise music under my uncle's eye. My greatest pleasure is, that both my uncle and aunt entirely approve of this arrangement which I have made; they enter into my motives as regards themselves, and were not only satisfied, but really affected by it. Their kindness to me is indescribable; were they my •wn parents, they could not show me more affection. In many respects, they remind me of my parents; in their attachment to each other, for instance, as well as in simplicity of character, and in uprightness and purity of mind.

"What a blessing is it, my dear friend, to be

descended from, and connected with, worthy people; people of whom one is proud, and with whom all that is good in one feels to be allied!

"*A week later.*—My letter is becoming a journal; but I have strange things to tell you.

"I was sitting two evenings ago at the piano, playing a beautiful sonata of Mozart's. My uncle said I played remarkably well, and I was unusually cheerful, for I had had a happy day with the children. The door opened, and our little maid-servant announced—a gentleman. Why, dear Mrs. Morland, did I feel ready to faint? God forgive me! I thought—but will not say of whom—and felt dizzy. It was Mr. Sopworth! Never was there a more awkward and constrained meeting. I thought of Barbara Pocklington; and I wondered why he was there. He sate, and we were all silent, for my uncle, it seems, had seen him before at W—, and had not liked him. I, for my part, felt as if I could not talk; I did not even ask him how you were. My aunt, who is the very soul of hospitality, and has a deal of natural politeness, did, as she said, double duty for us both. I never saw her so civil to anybody before; she talked of a hundred things, and asked a hundred questions, to all of which he gave short and broken answers.

"'Let us have some more music,' at length said my uncle, and then bade me play that sonata over again.

"Anything was better than that constrained silence in which we sate; so, though my heart beat almost audibly, I sate down and played. The magnificent instrument poured forth its volume of sound, and my uncle again greatly commended my playing. Mr. Sopworth rose the moment I had ended, and begged, in a low voice, that, if it were not convenient to be alone with me that evening, I would grant him an opportunity in the morning. 'I can see you but from eight to nine,' said I, with greater calmness than I thought myself capable; for, strange as it may seem, I felt there was no danger now of his troubling my peace of mind.

"My uncle and aunt were greatly disturbed by his visit; they, of course, believed him to be a lover; and my uncle, who, as I said before, had seen him at W——, began an earnest persuasion against him. They could not bear the thoughts of losing me; and neither of them were at all favourably impressed towards him.

"But you shall hear of our interview. I was not, I assure you, by any means so calm when we met again; my heart beat violently, a strange choking sensation made me feel as if I could not speak, and, catching a glimpse of myself in the glass, I saw that I was deadly pale. I suppose all these seemed to him favourable signs, for he began, almost confidently, to pour forth the most passionate avowal of love. Whilst he spoke I grew composed, and in a vein whose calmness quite astonished me I replied :—

" 'This time last year, or even six months ago, I might have listened to all this, and have believed it; and, if you then loved me as you say, why was such a declaration withheld? I was then extremely unhappy, wanted friends, wanted protectors, wanted

P

even a home ; my melancholy circumstances were
well known to you, for, in my misery, I in part
unfolded them to you. Then was the time to have
made offers of affection ; and, had you done so then,
I should almost have regarded you as an angel sent
from heaven !'

" He protested, he wept : and, oh Heavens ! there
are men whose weeping steels one's heart against
them. I felt almost indignant, and continued—
' You are accountable, Mr. Mark, to your own con-
science, and to God, for your actions ; but nevertheless, I demand from you, how you dare offer vows to
me, while you have already plighted them to another
—to Barbara Pocklington !'

" He shrunk back as if a serpent had stung him,
and then vehemently protested that he loved me far
better than her ; that he had always done so, that the
happiness of his life depended upon me, and that
nothing but obedience to his father's will would have
induced him to address her. He seemed almost
beside himself, and besought for my love and my
esteem.

" ' Time, and sickness, and knowledge of good and
noble hearts,' returned I, ' have made me see many
things in a very different light to what I did when
we were acquainted—in a very different light to that
in which you see them. Love I can never give you ;
the time for that is, thank God, long past ; and if my
esteem be of value to you, you should never have
presented yourself thus, with broken vows on your
lips, and falsehood to poor Barbara in your heart !'

" I was angry, and said many bitter things. I only

wonder he was not offended; but instead of that—which to my mind would, at least, have been manly,, he crouched like a beaten hound, and talked still of his love, and his broken heart. I was ashamed for him, and despised myself for having loved such a creature, especially as he said he had never had the courage to avow his love to me, and that his father compelled him to make love to Barbara against his own wishes.

"'Say not another word,' said I, rising, 'for a man that has not the heart to declare his love, does not deserve to have it returned; and he who could avow love to a girl, whilst that love is a lie to his own heart, is a despicable creature! You have signed your own death-warrant; and the very least that you can do—if there be the soul of a man in you—is to bear your punishment patiently. You have much to atone for to Barbara, in having thus deceived her! Return home, and endeavour to keep, if not to deserve, her love!'

"He left me. Thank Heaven! if my love were not cured before, it is perfectly cured now. This scene, however, has not been without its effects upon me. I am again suffering from headache, and my mind is not as calm, to perform its daily duties, as it ought to be.

"I feel out of spirits, and the sense, how very little we are fit to be the arbiters of our own destiny, weighs heavily upon me. I have lost somewhat of my own self-respect; for, only a few months since, and this was the man to whom I would have united myself! I will not, in future, set my mind on

anything. A good Providence disposes all things
aright; I will put myself in His hands, and leave all
to him.

"May God Almighty bless you! Your letters
always do me good, and no one sympathises so much
in your happiness and success, as your affectionate
and grateful   "MARY WHEELER."

Sopworth went home. No one, of course, knew
whither his journey had been directed, or what had
been the object of it. The news, however, which
greeted him on his return was, that old Mrs. Pocklington was ill, and that the family was in the greatest
distress. He felt ill himself; and, if he might have
followed the dictates of his own feelings, he would
have taken to his bed, and seen no human being;
but his sister hurried him to the home of his bride
elect, and, poor weak young man, it was no little
consolation to him, that the agitation which was
painted on his countenance might be mistaken, by
the Pocklington family, for anxiety on their account,
and natural sympathy with them.

Not a little surprised, of course, was Mrs. Morland by the contents of Mary's letter, but she
breathed not a syllable of it to any one. It was not
long, however, before a gossipping lady, who called
upon her, asked her if she had heard that the affair
was all at an end between Mark Sopworth and
Barbara Pocklington. Nobody, she said, justly knew
why; the mother was very ill—the family in great
distress, for she was both a good wife and good
mother; and that altogether, just at this time, it was

quite a shocking thing. It was, indeed, very strange, she continued, for the house was nearly ready; wedding-clothes were bought; and, as everybody knew, the marriage was to take place at Midsummer. Everybody, she said, was talking about it, but nobody could at all understand it!

So said rumour. In two weeks' time poor Mrs. Pocklington died, and the wedding could not now take place for the present, had the lovers been ever so amicable; but, strange to say, old Sopworth was at Mrs. Pocklington's funeral—Mark was not, because he was said to be ill, and confined to his bed; but when he was next seen in public, he was wearing mourning. "Oh," said rumour then, "there must have been nothing in the quarrel—Lizzy Sopworth was staying with Barbara Pocklington, and the two families were as friendly as ever; there must have been nothing in it; or if there were, it was only some trifling lovers' quarrel or other; but at a time like this, when the family was in such distress, all quarrels would be sure to be made up.

Mrs. Morland said nothing; she had no doubt whatever but that suspicion, if nothing more, of Mark's faithlessness had reached the Pocklingtons, which had occasioned a quarrel, and perhaps might have led to a total breach, had not that family sorrow softened and knit together all hearts, or had not Mark himself, perhaps, discovered some means of making his peace with them all.

P 2

CHAPTER XII.

ALL'S WELL THAT ENDS WELL.

THE summer wore cheerfully away. Nothing could have succeeded better than dear Mrs. Morland's management of her business. By Midsummer the superior quality of the articles she manufactured was acknowledged everywhere. Her husband, who had been twice at home for a whole week each time, declared that there was not a woman equal to her in all England, and that he grew more and more in love with her every day. The one pleasure which he had in life, he said, was the thought of the visit once a quarter which he should pay her; and the one sorrow was, that once a quarter he had to part from her. He did not buy nearly so many clothes for himself as formerly, although he appeared in new waistcoats each time he came; the one expense, however, which she had now to complain against was that of purchasing little presents for her. She tried to scold, but never was woman more pleased and flattered by presents than she was by his.

" What a lovely ring that is which you are wearing," said somebody to her one day.

" It is lovely," said she, " but its greatest beauty in my eyes is, that my husband gave it to me."

Mrs. Morland wrote to her uncle, and told him how successful she was in the business, and how happy she was besides as a wife. She told him that she should pay a hundred pounds of the borrowed money at Christmas; and at Christmas, she could not help telling him, that her husband would spend a whole fortnight with her, instead of a week; but she did not tell him, because she did not know, that he would then bring with him a hundred pounds which he, too, should have saved; she did not tell him this, because this was her husband's secret with himself —it was to be his Christmas present to her.

A happier woman than Mrs. Morland it would have been difficult to find; a better one, impossible. So her husband said every day of his life, never omitting to add, " and that for the life of him he never could tell how she ever came to marry a good-for-nothing dog like him!"

It was now August, and we must present our readers with a letter from Mary Wheeler to Mrs. Morland, written at two different dates.

" August 5th.

" All goes on well with me here.. My little pupils love me, and that is a great happiness; they make progress, too, and that pleases their parents, and keeps them in good humour with me. I find teaching agreeable, for the children learn readily, and I understand thoroughly what I have to teach.

" I begin to find that I make rapid advances in music; I understand and feel it much more than I used to do, and my uncle's encouragement and praise makes me happy.

" I must write to you again, of these dear old

people, and I thank you for encouraging me to do so, for every day unfolds some beautiful and amiable trait of character in them. I never could have imagined anything so perfect as the union of soul between them. She adores her husband, and without being slavishly imitative, she has adopted all his tastes and opinions, till they have come to harmonise together, like a fine accord in music. Their life has been without any great events, as calm as unruffled water; but the living soul within them has kept it from stagnation. Never regret, my dear friend, for yourself, that you are without family, or imagine that married life, under such circumstances, cannot be perfectly happy; my uncle and aunt had never children; they married young, and have lived together fifty years,—half a century of unbroken felicity, —what can human beings expect more?

" My uncle was a teacher of music; but his health, which suffered from confinement in a close town, induced them to retire to this village, where they hired a couple of rooms in the very house they now occupy, and hoped for the re-establishment of his health. This country life suited them both admirably; and a legacy which was left them of a small funded property, producing about eighty pounds a year, decided them upon settling down here for life. The occupant of the house, in the course of a few years, died, and they became its sole tenants, with no fear of ever being disturbed, because they had the good friendly squire, the father of the present one, for their landlord.

" The quiet and respectable life which they led,

together with his extraordinary talent for music, made him universally esteemed, and even courted; the squire's family, and the clergyman's, have always been his fast friends, and it was through his influence with them, that my father was appointed schoolmaster here. But this reminds me that I have not yet told you how many proofs I have had of the esteem in which my parents were held. In one cottage, I was shown a black profile likeness of my father, which was framed, and hung on the wall, and I was assured that nothing would induce them to part with it; and many a cottager and farmer has brought me little presents, because I was the daughter of my parents. I wish you could see the stand of hot-house plants, which one poor young man, a gardener, and a favourite pupil of my father's, brought me. With your love of flowers, you would be almost envious of them; they stand in a sunny window of the parlour, and, together with the piano, give an air of beauty, and a character of mind to the humble apartment.

" My uncle and aunt say, that I add greatly to their happiness; they lavish the greatest kindness upon me, and humour me like a child; yet, at the same time, my uncle pays me the greatest of all compliments, by consulting my taste and understanding. What a happiness it will be to have Ned here! I often talk of him, and his coming here, to the dear old people; but they seem to think that they shall never like him as they like me: that distresses me no little; but I am sure they will, and that again consoles me.

" My uncle is very particular about female dress,
I told you once how exquisitely neat my aunt always
was ; she is still more so, now that she has a servant, and, for an old person, dresses with a great
deal of feeling, if I may use such an expression.
My uncle likes best to see me in white, and I would
wear it always, as I too think it becoming, were
it not for the washing ; but, as my aunt pays for
the getting up of my dresses out of the house, I am
extremely careful.   Every Sunday, however, while
the weather is so fine, I put on a clean frock, and
you may fancy me, if you will, in such a dress, a
black silk scarf, the present of my aunt, and a white
chip bonnet, plainly trimmed, and with pink roses
inside,—a dress which pleases both myself and my
uncle ; see me then, thus apparelled, walking out
with the two dear old people, on these fine evenings,
or on a Sunday afternoon ; my aunt leaning on his
arm ; she rather handsomely dressed in black silk ;
the least in the world vain, dear old soul ! of a foot
and hand remarkably small and well made, and
which are always well gloved and well shod.   See
us walking up the village, and here a cottager runs
out with a little nosegay of flowers for us, and there,
a little girl courtesys to us as we pass ; and now, the
clergyman's servant is sent out to invite us in to eat
a little fruit, which shall be freshly gathered for us ;
and now, one farmer's wife begs us to come in and
take tea, and another, to eat a syllabub fresh from
the cow ; and thus, wherever we turn, we find
friends and kindness.   The fat schoolmaster has
to-day sent us a present of vegetable marrows ; and

yesterday, a poor cottager, who has a remarkably fine peach-tree, the fruit of which he sends to the town to sell, sent us a dozen peaches in a little basket, by his two youngest children. The children were pretty, and were dressed as carefully for the occasion as if they had been going to the squire's instead. I cannot tell you how this little proof of regard pleased and affected me. I did not give the children money, for that would have been like stripping the gift of its charm; but I kissed the children, and my aunt crammed into their hands, each a great hunch of seed-cake, for which she is as famous now as when we were children; and I, who took also the measure of the children in my eye, will make each of them a warm winter frock, out of my old blue merino.

"I have this moment received your letter, and what you say of my poor uncle Crawley almost reproaches me for thinking so much of my own happiness. I am really distressed for him; I thought his bankruptcy would have delivered him from a jail. Alas! to be 'sick and in prison!' that is mentioned in the Gospel as one of the most grievous afflictions of human nature. I have two guineas which I will send him, if you will undertake to let them reach his hands; by the first opportunity I will send them to you, but in the meantime, lose no time in relieving him. Do not say that they come from me; I dare not establish any claim upon me, for I may not always have it in my power to help him; say that they come from one who wishes him well.

" I take up my pen again, but I am hardly in a
state to write. I am happy—indescribably happy
—happy beyond the power of words to express.
Last night, when I was alone in my chamber, I fell
on my knees, and would have blessed God, but
I had no words; I laid my face on my hands and
wept, and the Almighty, who can read all hearts,
saw what was in mine. But I must not longer keep
you in suspense; and yet I must be circumstantial.

" Listen, then :—After tea last evening, instead of
allowing me to sit down to my music during daylight, my aunt insisted upon my taking a walk.
My uncle was gone up to the other end of the
village, to the house of the organist, to play to that
poor youth of whom I told you before. He had
been gone a couple of hours, and my aunt thought
that if I walked in that direction I should meet him,
and thus we two might take a walk together. It
was Monday, and I had my Sunday dress on. The
evening was heavenly, warm and bright, and some
way or other I felt a more than ordinary pleasure in
all around me, and, I know not why, dressed myself
with particular care—never thinking what was about
to happen! But I will not proceed too fast. I have
a pleasure in dwelling on every little circumstance of
that happy evening.

" One of the little children who brought us the
present of the peaches, was going up the village with
a basket on her arm ; she was as neat and clean as
when she came to us, and I thought she was going
to the rector's, or perhaps to the squire's.

"'And where are you going, Patty?' said I.

"She looked up at me so good and happy, and lifted the lid of her basket; there was a little cake in it, and a pair of new woollen stockings. 'I am taking the cake to granny,' said she; 'mother has baked to-day, and Jane' (that was her eldest sister, out at service), 'has sent granny this pair of stockings that she has knit herself; so I am going to her with them!'

"It was quite a happiness to me to hear of so much family affection and good will; my heart blessed them all, and I gave the little girl a sixpence for herself. She looked as happy as I myself felt, and trudged on before me almost conceitedly, with a pair of stiff little legs in black worsted stockings, that some way or other quite charmed me. .

"When I reached the organist's, my uncle was not there; he had been gone a quarter of an hour, and as nobody could tell me exactly in which direction he had gone, and the evening was so lovely, I determined to go onward to the cottage of the old grandmother, and see if she were not greatly pleased with the presents which the little child had brought her. It was about a quarter of a mile further to her cottage, along one of the loveliest lanes you can imagine ; the fields were full of harvesters cutting the corn, who were laughing and singing as I went along; the sound of ringing bells came on the air from a not far-off village; the evening sunshine cast a glow over everything, like burnished gold ; a foreboding of happiness filled my heart, and, saying to myself that there was far more good than evil in life after all, I went onward. The

Q

old grandmother had put on her new stockings when
I got there, and was delighted to have somebody to
show them to, and was altogether as full of satisfaction as I was myself. I had another sixpence in my
pocket, and gave it to her—in return for which she
made me up a nosegay of stocks and china-asters;
and, well pleased with my little visit, as you may
believe, I set out again on my homeward way.

"Just as I reached the top of the village, I saw
before me, coming towards me, and at about a hundred yards distance—now I wish I could keep you
waiting before I tell you who I saw; for, happy as I
am, I have a pleasure in toying, as it were, with my
happiness—I saw Dr. Wentworth coming towards
me, and looking as if he rejoiced in this meeting.

" I don't know really what he said, or how I came
to understand and believe that he was come purposely
to Morton to see me—that he had seen both my uncle
and aunt, and had set out wilfully alone to meet me,
and that I must take his arm, and walk with him,
and listen to what he had to say.

" What he said exactly I really do not know: I
only know that after the sun had set and the full
moon had risen, we were both standing together,
leaning against a gravestone in the churchyard—the
gravestone of my father and mother—and that never
in this world did human being feel happier than I
did. I could say nothing, however; I could only
wish that I could kneel down and bless the Almighty
Father for his goodness to me. I thought of my
parents, who had lived so in love together, and were
now sleeping below that turf side by side; my hand

was clasped in that of the man whom, above all others, I honoured and esteemed in this world. He was talking to me ; but though his voice was like music in my ears, I know not exactly what he said, excepting that he spoke of love—eternal love !

" The purple light of evening had quite died away, and the moon shone brilliantly in the cloudless heaven, as, leaning on his arm, we walked slowly homeward. It seemed to me as if the cup of my earthly felicity were brimming full, and I feared to breathe almost, lest it should run over. I was so full of happiness, that I could not say one word, but felt subdued and still ; he, on the contrary, seemed almost wild—nor could I have thought it possible that he could be so much excited.

" I called him Dr. Wentworth ; he told me never to call him so again, but Herbert, which was his Christian name.

" ' Herbert Wentworth,' repeated I to myself, ' it is a beautiful name !' but, like all that belongs to him, it is superior to the rest of the world. Tell me, dearest friend, is it not so ?

" When we got home we found my uncle and aunt ready to receive us. Dear old people ! they never for one moment imagined what was his errand ; but for all that, my aunt had got supper ready, all so neatly set out ; her best table-cloth on her table, and a bottle of her best wine on it too. My uncle had opened his music-book at his favourite piece, by Beethoven, which he meant to play that evening to the Doctor. I went into my own room to take off my things, and when I returned, my uncle and aunt came forward, each seizing a hand of mine, and kissing me tenderly, for Dr. Wentworth had told them all.

" I never was so silent in my life. I thought I must be stupid not to talk, but that overpowering happiness had chained my tongue.

" ' Well, if she will not talk,' said my uncle quite merrily, ' she must\play to us ; she can play very tolerably, Dr. Wentworth,' said he, laying aside the Beethoven, and opening at that sonata of Mozart's, which he reckoned my masterpiece.

" I played ; Dr. Wentworth turned over the pages of my music-book ; but oh ! never did I play so badly in all my life before. My uncle grew almost angry, and seating himself at the piano, played magnificently. Our little parlour reverberated the almost deafening sounds, for my uncle was doing his grandest ; my aunt was enchanted with his performance, and we two sat side by side on the little sofa his arm round my waist, and my head resting upon his bosom.

" Congratulate me now, for am I not happy—am I not fortunate ? Oh, Almighty Father, how can I have deserved such unspeakable happiness !

" I have, my dear friend, written this long letter during his absence for a few hours to visit a college friend of his some few miles off. I have begged for myself a holiday for to-day. This evening he returns, and to-morrow he leaves us.

" Many things seem strange, and yet not incomprehensible to me either. When in the early year, Dr. Wentworth proposed to me first, how astonished I was! my foolish heart was then unworthily pre-occupied. I was rudely shaken out of that dream, and passed through a baptism both deep and painful: but if I suffered, I acquired knowledge cheaply bought by suffering—knowledge of myself, and a truer estimate of others. In the six ensuing months, I had become, I trust, worthier of my destiny; I understood and appreciated more thoroughly a character and virtues like those of Dr. Wentworth. Love for him I certainly did not cherish, because I had no hope; but excellence like his seemed to be that after which I was striving; and thus, when we now met, it seemed to me that we had been in constant communion ever since. He seemed to me like an old friend whom I knew intimately, and I could have no reserves with him. I have opened my whole heart to him, for I desire to conceal nothing, and in him I have confidence the most undoubting.

"People talk of happiness being extatic; to me it is a still and inward feeling. I have all I wish for, and I do not fear change. The reality of heaven must be like this!

"He is returned; farewell, dearest friend! He will take this with him. I enclose, too, the two guineas for my uncle. Once again, farewell!

"M. W."

THE END.

www.ingramcontent.com/pod-product-compliance
Lightning Source LLC
Chambersburg PA
CBHW020541270326
41927CB00006B/675